Hamlyn ◆ paperbacks

Cyril Rogers FBSA

Pet Birds

illustrated by Peter Morter
& Design Bureau

Hamlyn - London
Sun Books - Melbourne

FOREWORD

Birds as pets, either singly or collectively, have given and will continue to give a tremendous amount of friendly companionship and pleasure to their human owners. This book has been designed to give the reader an idea of the vast number of varieties of birds that can be kept as pets. The reader will realize that, with such a wide field, only a limited number of examples of the various species could be discussed. These have been specially selected as their general treatment, feeding and management are applicable to related members of their group. For those who require further information about particular kinds of birds, a list of specialist books will be found at the end of the volume.

I would like to thank my wife for her great help in dealing with the various aspects of birds in the home and also Peter Morter for his most excellent illustrations of birds and the many aspects of their keeping.

C.R.

Published by the Hamlyn Publishing Group Limited
London · New York · Sydney · Toronto
Hamlyn House, Feltham, Middlesex, England
In association with Sun Books Pty Ltd Melbourne

Copyright © The Hamlyn Publishing Group Limited 1970

ISBN 0 600 00102 4
Photoset by BAS Printers Limited, Wallop, Hampshire
Colour separations by Schwitter Limited, Zurich
Printed in Holland by Smeets, Weert

CONTENTS

INTRODUCTION

'When were birds first kept as pets or companions by man?'
is a question that is often asked. As far as it is possible to
ascertain, they were kept long before picture, or elementary,
writing was used. There are also records that show that, in the
very ancient civilizations of both the Old and New Worlds,
birds were to be found in human communities. Carved
inscriptions show that the Egyptians kept many kinds of pet
birds including song birds, parrots, doves, ducks and ibis.
Several species of hawk were used for hunting wildfowl and
members of the nobility were frequently depicted in hunting
scenes with hawks on their arms or being carried by their
slaves.

Chinese pottery, carvings and silk paintings, also show
birds of various kind being kept as domestic pets. The ancient

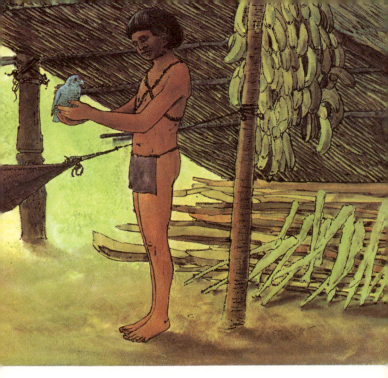

South American Indians with a Festive Amazon Parrot (*Amazona festiva*). This bird is very easy to tame but not much of a talker.

Incas of South America tamed many kinds of birds and kept them in their houses, palaces and temples. Ancient Britons caught and tamed native species for their song or for use in the hunting field. In fact it would seem that birds of different kinds are probably man's oldest household pets and close companions.

The pages that follow try to show, by text and illustrations how pet bird keeping can be interesting and entertaining. A lot, of course, depends on the kind of treatment birds receive from their owners. Obviously many people are restricted by circumstances as to the kind of bird they can keep, and the conditions necessary for a bird's happy life must be studied closely before any particular pet is selected.

Early English illustration showing hawking. The sport is of undoubted antiquity and was introduced into Britain by the Normans.

HISTORY

When early men led a nomadic existence, wandering from place to place in search of food, the keeping of birds especially as pets could have found little favour amongst them. These peoples lived mainly by hunting and it can therefore be deduced that the first birds they were attracted to were the hawks, because these birds too were great hunters.

From these very early times hawks of many kinds were carefully trained to hunt wildfowl and other game for their owners. The nomadic races must have been the earliest bird-keepers with their trained hunting hawks, and it seems very unlikely that they attempted to keep any other kind of bird, whether they roamed over temperate or tropical areas.

When these nomadic races started to live in small settlements and villages they made stone carvings and wall paintings showing the prowess of their favourite hunting birds.

Geese as illustrated by an Egyptian frieze. Waterfowl were provided with ornamental lakes in the grounds of houses and temples.

Then they began to realize that other birds had an even greater potential as a source of food and the number of hawks kept in captivity began to decline.

The face of the world has changed much since those early times but there are still people who keep and train hawks and falcons for the purpose of hunting. Records can date this association with man back for over five thousand years. The reason they were first attracted to these birds of prey was as a means of procuring food and only later for their own personal pleasure and sport. Two terms used in hawking are still employed in the English language today; these are a 'hawker' and a 'cadger'. Originally the hawker was one who travelled around the country peddling trained hawks. The cadger, who carried the frame for the hooded birds was the humblest servant of the chase and, ever since then, the name has been a term of reproach.

Another quite different kind of bird that has been kept in

In China and Japan cormorants have been used for fishing for centuries. The birds are prevented from swallowing by a thong, close around the neck.

captivity by the Chinese for a great many centuries is the fishing cormorant. These birds are captured when very young and are tamed and then trained to catch fish for their owners. The birds are prevented from swallowing the fish they catch by a band fixed around their necks, so that the fish remain in their mouths. A long tether keeps them attached to the boat. Here again man's interest in keeping these cormorants was motivated by their ability to work for their owners in catching fish for food and for trade.

Since the dawn of history the birds we now call domestic poultry have been kept as utilitarian pets by various races of men, because they were good food themselves and in addition could produce eggs in captivity. When the vast range of different varieties and shapes of the domesticated poultry of today is examined it will clearly be seen that most of them are a far cry from the small jungle fowls that were their common ancestors.

It can be seen from the above brief notes that man's first contact with birds had one basic reason – food. The exact period of time when birds came to be kept in captivity solely for pleasurable reasons is difficult to ascertain accurately. It is thought that with the advances of the different civilizations birds of various kind were kept in captivity so that man could enjoy the pleasure of their song and colours at close quarters. A number of ancient books, including the Bible, mention birds as friends and companions of human beings. For many ages doves have been singled out as a world-wide symbol of peace, here again showing the deep human regard for bird life.

The ancient Egyptians kept waterfowl and other water-loving birds in specially constructed and ornamented lakes and pools in the gardens of the nobility and in the precincts of the temples of their numerous gods and goddesses. The falcon, Horus or Shahoun, the god of Pharaoh, is the oldest

Dayak (*right*) holds a cock Red Jungle Fowl (*Gallus gallus*), which is the ancestor of all domestic poultry. The association with man has been a long one and Asiatic records date back some 3,000 years.

of the idols and its huge black granite effigy among the columns of Edfu is extraordinarily life-like. They also constructed aviaries to house colourful song birds and parrot-like species in the mansions of prominent families. Doves and pigeons of various kinds were kept and allowed complete freedom of the houses and surrounding estates.

The early Indian Princes and notables must have been some of the very first actual breeders of birds in captivity, as they constructed elaborate aviaries for housing parrot-like and other exotic birds. They had special servants to look after and tend their stocks of birds, which were often rated far more valuable than human beings.

Most probably the ancient Egyptian traders brought back to their native land the Indian's idea of keeping birds in aviaries. It is known that live birds, mainly of the parrot-like species, often formed part of their trading consignments with that part of the world. Alexander the Great was the first person to import Ring-necked Parrakeets into Europe. He

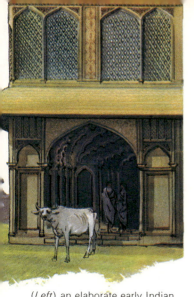

(*Left*) an elaborate early Indian aviary that would have housed their exotic birds. Special servants were entrusted with their care. (*Below*) a Wild Canary (*Serinus canaria*), which comes from the Canary Islands and measures $5\frac{1}{2}$ inches.

first saw the birds on his travels in India and brought some back with him when he returned to Greece.

Monks of the Middle Ages were known to be great animal lovers and it is highly probable that members of European brotherhoods took cage birds with them to their new homes. They kept these for pleasure as well as to study their way of life.

It was in the fifteenth and sixteenth centuries that native song birds began to be fairly widely kept as pets in both mansion and cottage in Britain, and for that matter most of the continent of Europe. Today the keeping of pet birds of many kinds has become an integral part of the everyday life of most civilized communities.

One of the seed-eating birds much prized for its sweet song was a small, yellowish-green finch-type bird, the common ancestor of all the different kinds of caged birds that are today called Canaries. It would seem from old ornithological writings that during the fifteenth century the Spani-ards first started to breed these birds in captivity and thus started the process of their domestication.

The keeping and breeding of Canaries, as they were latterly called, steadily began to spread all over Europe, and different colours and type forms began to emerge. In Victorian times a caged Canary, or some other singing bird, was often to be found hanging in many windows of small houses and cottages both in town and country.

Although wild Canaries are to be found living on the Canary Islands, they did not originate there. The legend of how Canaries came to the Canary Islands is an interesting one and is most probably true to a certain extent. It would seem that a Spanish sailing vessel making for the Port of Leghorn, carrying in its cargo some cages of Canaries, ran into bad weather and started to sink. While the sailors were getting into the boats, a bird-lover among them liberated the Canaries from their cages, hoping they would make landfall safely. Since the wind was in the right direction, it enabled at least some of the birds to reach the Islands, now known as the Canary Islands. Here they found the food and water

(*Below*) Canaries did not originate in the Canary Islands although they are supposed to have given these islands their name.
(*Right*) a Victorian drawing-room with tame Budgerigars

plentiful and weather conditions most suitable and settled down to raising families. At the present time there are thriving colonies of wild Canaries populating various parts of the Islands.

Although there is a whole range of different colours and shapes of Canaries existing at the present time, all are descended from the little, wild, yellowish-green birds. Strangely enough, although at one time they were so very favoured by pet-keepers they now take second place to another domesticated bird, the Budgerigar. This change of favour is really understandable as the actual colours and variations existing in Budgerigars are innumerable and they also have the attraction of the gift of mimicry.

Budgerigars are really quite new as caged birds, only having been seen in captivity for the first time in Great Britain in 1840. Since then, these friendly little birds have been bred most freely in all parts of the world and during that period have given a multitude of new and lovely colours by the process of mutation. These new colour phases have been cultivated by keen and skilful breeders, who have increased their number of colour combinations to a fantastic degree. With all this in their favour it is easy to see why Budgerigars have claimed the hearts of so many people all over the world.

Sailors were frequently respon-
sible for bringing exotic birds,
such as this Spot-billed Toucan,
from the tropical regions.

Back in the days of sailing ships, parrot-like birds were
invariably associated with seafaring men, and different
species were to be found for sale at ports in Britain and in
Europe wherever ships from tropical or semi-tropical parts
berthed. These sailors obtained their birds from the natives
of those distant lands, who had for generations caught, and
trained, parrot-like birds, and sometimes offered them for
sale or trade. In the ancient civilizations of South America,
various birds were kept as pets and in fact were a part of
their way of life. Many of the first parrots that came to
Europe came from this area.

During the old Chinese and Japanese empires, numerous
species of birds were kept as pets and these included both

seed-eating and soft-feeding song birds and various water fowl and game. Many of these species are often depicted in paintings on silk, porcelain and china and carved in wood, jade, ivory and soapstone.

It was in this part of the world that the very first domesticated caged bird was evolved. The exact history of these birds, now known as Bengalese Finches, is not really clear. It is known, however, that they were produced by eastern bird-breeders from the crossing together of several small Mannikins, and then selectively breeding from them to get a range of different colours.

The latest species of bird to become fully domesticated in Britain is the Zebra Finch which has now some half-dozen colour mutations. This little Australian finch was first declared to be domesticated in 1958 by a Society formed for its development. A considerable number of British birds are now constantly bred in captivity and several species are progressing towards becoming fully domesticated. By this means it is hoped to be able to preserve some species that might be threatened by extinction.

The following chapters in this book will be devoted to the overall general management of birds that can be taken fully as household pets, and those considered as outside pets because of their size or unsuitability for living in a house.

Various coloured forms of the Zebra Finch (*Taniopygis castanotis*) from Australia, $4\frac{1}{4}$ inches

POPULAR CAGE BIRDS

Canaries

For over 400 years Canaries have been household pets in most countries of the world. Their sweet song has given pleasure to millions of people of all races and ages, both in sickness and in health. Their popularity is due to a great extent to their ease of feeding and keeping, and because the cages which house them take up little space. With care and patience on the part of their owners they will become very attractive pets, quite finger-tame and fearless, and their life expectancy is very good indeed.

This tame Border Canary is one of the most popular breeds and occurs in a variety of colours.

The name Canary invariably brings to mind the vision of a small, yellow-coloured bird in a decorative, all-wire cage. Although many Canaries are one of the shades of yellow in colour they also come in other colour forms ranging from green, like the original Canary, to red-orange and pastel shades. They can be of all one colour or they can be variegated such as yellow and green, green and white, white and fawn, or orange and cinnamon, to mention some of the possible combinations of colours.

In addition to all these various colours, Canaries are bred

Canaries have been bred as pets for over 400 years. This sort of cage may well have been hung in drawing-room windows.

in different shapes and sizes all of which breed true to their own particular type. Although all these type Canaries, as they are called, can sing quite well, they are each called by a special name to distinguish them from the pure singing Canaries known as Roller Canaries. These latter birds are bred solely for the purity of their song notes, their colour and shape being of no vital importance, whereas with the type Canaries shape and colour are the prominent features with the singing capabilities being secondary. On pages 26 to 27 there is a list of the different breeds of Canaries, together with a brief description, so that each kind can be recognized.

It will be realized that, as with the majority of species of birds, it is only the cocks that sing to any extent, the hens just having a variation of call and alarm notes. However, with a few breeds of Canaries some hen birds do sing a little, and all of them with training will become very tame and friendly towards their owner.

As a general rule, one of the smaller breeds of Canary such as a Border Fancy, Gloster Fancy, Red Factor, Roller or one of their crosses, is the best single household pet. These varieties can all be had in a variation of colour forms, so that, if the colour of the bird is particularly important, the intended owner has quite a wide choice of birds. It should be noted, however, that the colour of the bird does not in any way influence its ability to sing.

When a selected breed of Canary is to be kept as a pet it is always best to get a young bird, and preferably an un-moulted one. There are two main reasons for doing this. The first is that such a bird will settle down to its new owner's management much more easily than an older bird and consequently will become tamer in a shorter space of time. The other reason for getting a young bird is that it gives the longest possible time for it to be a lively companion to its owner. As the breeding of Canaries is generally carried out during the spring and early summer months, it is obvious that the best time to buy a pet bird is during the late summer and early autumn.

Before a bird is actually bought it is necessary for the prospective owner to have everything in readiness for the reception of the new pet. This means getting a cage and having a supply of food and other items that are needed for the bird's well-being on hand. The type of cage that is provided can vary considerably but the all-wire cage is the one that will show the bird off to the best advantage. It should be mentioned here that cages made of a combination of clear plastic and wire can be had, but although these are attractive they may not be so easy for some owners. If an all-wire cage is used it should be kept in a place free from draughts. If this is not possible then a more sheltered box-type cage should be provided, or part of the all-wire cage covered over to give protection. In addition to the fitted seed and water vessels, a small separate pot for grit and a holder for cuttlefish bone will be needed.

(*Right*) suitable present-day cage for the young pet Border Canary the owner holds in his hand. The cuttlefish bone and grit provide essential minerals for the bird's general well-being.

Bowl of grit

Cuttlefish bone in
its special holder

All fancy, wire cages are fitted with a movable tray at the bottom, and this can be covered with either bird sand or specially prepared, sanded paper sheets. The use of either of these is a matter of personal preference, but if bird sand is used it gives the bird an extra opportunity to get grit and other minerals, necessary for its well-being. Really the best method is to use the sanded sheets, which are easy to remove when soiled, and scatter over it a small amount of grit which the bird can pick up easily.

To help minimize the amount of seed husks, grit or green food falling on to the floor of the home, special plastic cage bottom covers can be obtained. These will catch husks and other material and can be emptied as desired. They are made in different sizes and of various colours and look quite attractive, as well as being practical.

Canaries, like most birds, take a bath several times a week and should be given the opportunity to do so. As can be imagined, during bath-time water is splashed around quite

Outdoor aviary with a selection of coloured Yorkshires, Norwich and Borders. (*Below*) a bird bath that can be fixed over the door of a cage

a lot. To make the inconvenience to the owner as slight as possible, specially designed baths in both plastic or metal and glass can be obtained. These baths fit over the open door of the cage and are protected on three sides and the top so that little or no water can be splashed into the room.

Although as a rule Canaries do not appreciate the number of playthings that Budgerigars do, some of them do find amusement in a small mirror. This and the accessories mentioned above can all be obtained from good pet shops.

Some people like to keep more than one bird, and a small pen or large cage of Canaries on a terrace or loggia, or in a summer house or glass house make an attractive show. Kept under such conditions a small flock of Canaries of one or more variety can be most colourful and entertaining to the owner and to visitors.

When batches of Canaries are housed together it is usual to allow three hen birds to each cock bird. This prevents undue fighting and the birds will usually manage to raise a number of vigorous chicks each year.

Fit healthy stock are quite hardy and can stand cold winters without additional heat, providing they have dry and draught proof sleeping quarters. Fresh water must be supplied every day and birds have been known to have a bath when they are given fresh water even though the temperature may have been well below freezing. If a shallow dish of tepid water is put into the cage of a pet bird for it to bath in just before the cage is cleared out then it will not matter if water is splashed on to the floor.

Yorkshire Wing-marked Buff, 6¾ inches

The actual size of the pen or large cage depends on the number of birds that are to be housed in comfort. On no account should there be any attempt at squeezing too many birds together, if so, the happy, contented state of the stock of Canaries will be badly upset. If a fairly large number of birds are to be kept together then nothing can be better than a decorative outside aviary with an all wire front. Adequate provision for cleaning is important in these types of aviary and an entrance must be made into the main flight area and

Border Canary, 5½ inches

also the enclosed sheltered area at the back where the birds usually sleep. The same ratio of hens to cocks as for pens should be carried out in a flight aviary, that is, three hen birds to each cock bird.

Whether one has a single pet, a small pen or an aviary of Canaries, they all need the same feeding arrangements. To keep the birds fit and healthy they must be provided with a good seed mixture of canary seed and sweet red rape as their diet. When a large number of birds are kept, a good all round mixture can be made up of one part large canary seed, two parts small canary and one part sweet red rape. For a single pet bird it is usually more convenient to buy already packaged seeds. During spells of cold weather a little hemp seed, nigar seed and linseed can be added to the above mixture to provide an increase in the heat-giving natural oil.

Norwich Clear Yellow, 6-6½ inches

In addition to the standard mixture of bird-seed, Canaries will benefit by periodically having some mixed, wild weed seeds, perhaps once a week. These wild seeds contain a whole host of various weed seeds, which contain different quantities of essential vitamins. Packets of these mixed seeds can usually be obtained from most pet shops.

Green food and fruit are also essential for supplying the birds with the necessary elements for their well-being. Canaries are particularly partial to seeding Chickweed, seeding grasses, although not the hairy kind, and the seeding heads of Shepherd's Purse, Plantain and Sowthistle. Young tender Dandelion leaves, Spinach and heart of Cabbage are also very acceptable. Of the fruits they seem to prefer sweet apples and pears, but some pet birds have a great liking for a small piece of banana or half a grape. Periodically a small dish of one of the patent cod liver oil soft foods

Suitable Canary green foods :
1. Shepherds Purse seeds
2. Marram Grass seed
3. Sowthistle
4. Plantain
5. Fescue Grass seed
6. Young Dandelion leaves

Two Gloster Fancy Canaries. These are birds that are rapidly rising in popularity among owners. They are quite small measuring 4¾ inches in length.

can be given to the benefit of the birds and this is particularly important at moulting times and when they have young.

When supplying the birds with greenstuffs, care should be taken to see that it is fresh and clean. The source should be examined carefully to see if it has been fouled in any way, the food washed under plenty of running water and then partially dried before it is given to the birds. In winter frosted foods must be specially avoided as they are very dangerous, causing stomach troubles often with fatal results.

It is very essential that pet Canaries, and in fact all Canaries, however housed, should have a constant supply of mixed grits, a piece of cuttlefish bone, and a mineral nibble. These are most important to supply the birds with the means of assimilating their food and providing them with the necessary trace elements for their well-being.

Although a pet Canary will usually be found in a room in a house, this does not mean that a pet bird cannot travel or

Many pet birds can be moved around without being disturbed by their change of surroundings. Owners often take their pets with them on holiday.

be moved about. Some owners are quite prepared to take their pets with them when they go away on holiday. The cage can be placed on the front or back seat of a car and will be quite safe and the bird should be quite unconcerned about the movement. If it does appear to be fretful a cloth over the cage should stop the pet being worried during the journey. Usually pets seem to benefit from the change of air.

Although there seem to be numerous colours, shapes and sizes of Canaries there are basically only a few breeds which, if mated together, all breed true to their type. These can all be related back to their wild ancestor, of course, but because of consistent breeding of mutations, the following types that vary considerably in body form and often in colour, have been produced.

Border Canaries are neat, compact, cleanly feathered birds of $5\frac{1}{2}$ inches in overall length. The most popular of all the breed Canaries, they are to be had in yellow (buff), green, cinnamon, white, blue, fawn, variegated and dilute colours.

Norwich Canaries are birds of much heavier build overall and 6 to 6½ inches in length. They can be had in the same colours as the Border Canaries with the exception of dilute. **Yorkshire Canaries** are very long slender birds, heavier at the shoulders and 6¾ inches in overall length. They have the same colourings as Norwich Canaries.

Gloster Canaries are another neat and compact breed, slightly smaller than the Border, being 4¾ inches in overall length. These can be had with or without a small neat head crest and are coloured as the Border.

Lizard Canaries are a very old breed with delightful ticked pattern markings and a clear head. The length is 5 inches overall. The colours here are gold (yellow), silver (buff) and blue.

Roller Canaries are thick birds similar to the Border type, but slightly shorter in length. Although colour is not important as these are song birds, they can be had in all usual shades of colour.

Red Factor Canaries are small slender birds of about 4¾ inches in overall length and with a strong Siskin-like shape. They can be bred in shades of orange to deep red.

Clear Cap Gold Lizard, 5 inches

Red Factor Canary, 4¾ inches

Mules

Quite often people who are not very familiar with the different colours and colour patterns of Canaries think that when they see a green and yellow, or cinnamon and yellow Canary, such birds are the result of crossing Canaries with other birds. In most cases this assumption is incorrect and the bird in

Goldfinch cock

Border Canary hen

question is just one of the variegated breeds and, in fact, a pure Canary. However there are numerous birds that are bred each year from crossings of a Canary and one of the finches such as the Goldfinch, Linnet, Greenfinch or Bullfinch. Birds resulting from these parents are known generally as Canary Mules and they are mostly sterile.

Mules are usually bred for exhibition purposes with the main aim of achieving either a clear yellow like a Canary but with the finch shape and characters, or a wholly dark bird showing a paler finch colour pattern and shape. This results, of course, in a large number of mules being bred with broken coloured plumage and from these come many household pets.

As singing pets, mules are excellent and will become very tame and friendly with their owner. They also have an attractive range of song notes and their song will vary according to the kind of finch that was one of their parents. Because of their rather pretty colour arrangement Goldfinch mules are probably the most popular as pets and their song is very sweet indeed. Although more sombre in their colouring, the Linnet mules have an excellent singing tone and therefore find much favour as pets with people who realize that they have this particular asset.

Mules need the same general treatment and housing as pure Canaries, except that their standard seed mixture should be about half Canary seed with the balance made up of mixed finch seeds. A suitable mixture for mules can be bought at all good pet shops.

They are exceedingly fond of all kinds of green foods and particularly like the half-ripe seeding heads of most garden weeds. They also require grit, cuttlefish bone, and mineralized blocks and, like the Canary, they are also fond of bathing.

Crossing between a Canary and one of the finch species often produces very interesting and attractive pets. (*Below from top to bottom*) Goldfinch, Linnet and Bullfinch mules

Hybrids

The birds known in the Cage Bird Fancy as mules are the result of crossing together a Canary and a finch, but in addition to these crosses, there are also crosses between two actual finches. Like the mules these hybrid Finches are bred mainly for the purposes of exhibition. While this is the main object, a few birds who lack some of the essential show properties are disposed of as pets. Because of their cross-parentage many of them have a most unusual colour arrangement and, consequently, are extremely attractive. Their song notes are also mixed, but pure finch-like in tone and, therefore, can be very harmonious. Although not all hybrids are really good as pets because of their restless nature, nevertheless, some birds really do settle down. When they do so they

Bullfinch/Goldfinch hybrid

Bullfinch hen

Goldfinch cock

are extremely interesting and entertaining and make first-class household pets.

They can be housed in the usual, all-wire decorative cage that is used for the pet Canary or mule, but they must have a good finch seed mixture with the other usual items that are needed for their well-being. Like the mules they are extremely fond of green food and seeding weed heads and should always have a supply to keep them fit, healthy and happy.

Both mules and hybrids, once they have settled down to the life of a household pet and are well fed on a good plain seed and not given unnecessary tit-bits, will live and delight their owner for many years. They seem to have an extra long life expectation, which is usually only rivalled by that of the popular Budgerigar.

Redpoll hen

Redpoll/Siskin hybrid

Siskin cock

Housing

The principle method of housing pet Canaries, mules or hybrids, is the fancy decorative cage which can be obtained in great variety at all good pet shops. The cages can be of the plain hanging type or those with a stand, and which kind is bought depends on the situation where the bird is to be mainly kept. If there are other household pets, such as cats or dogs, then the cage and stand would seem the safest way of housing a pet bird. In certain circumstances, for example where there are draughts, a box-type cage, one that is made of wood except for the front which is wire, is best.

A home-made box-type cage is relatively simple to construct since the punch-bar wire fronts can be bought at any pet shop. It must be possible to remove the complete front, if necessary, for cleaning.

Whatever cage is selected, it should be made of good, sound material and, if possible, one that will not rust or deteriorate in any way. The perches should be kept to a minimum, so that the bird will have the maximum amount of exercise room. The perches themselves should be of different thicknesses. The food, water and grit vessels should be simple and straightforward, so their cleaning is easy. Once the bird is tame and allowed the liberty of a room, a ledge fixed to the open door will facilitate its entrance and exit to the cage.

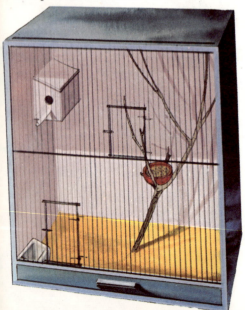

This box cage has a nesting box and natural wood perches. There are access doors into both parts of the cage since it is much larger than the one above.

All-wire cages are more attractive for keeping birds in the house and they frequently have their own stand (*below*) or suspension hook so that they can be hung in a window or place of safety.

The construction of a larger cage or small pen to take several birds is again a matter of space available and the owner's particular fancy. The importance of not overcrowding the birds should be stressed and an allowance of some 4 cubic feet per bird should be made.

Large cages can be made partly of wood and partly of wire, and the wire can be either wire netting, the newer square welded mesh, or punch bar panels, which can be bought in varying sizes. These panels have doors and drinker holes, which can be utilized to advantage. In the case of a small pen, this can again be made of wood and square welded mesh wire and can be constructed to fit in almost any odd-shaped corner. Cages or pens should be so constructed that the owner can reach every part. The decoration should be simple and the inside woodwork given a good coating of emulsion paint. Any woodwork which may have an outside surface should be given several coats of creosote, wood preservative, or paint, according to its position.

In these structures food, grit and water vessels will naturally be larger than those in a house cage, and the perches can be made of fruit tree branches and arranged tastefully. The perches should not be positioned directly over the food, water or grit vessels, or fouling will occur. The floor can be covered with a good washed sand or a mixture of sand and coarse pine sawdust.

If the owner has decided to keep a number of Canaries in a decorative aviary, the design again should be simple with just a shelter and a wired flight. An aviary structure can be a new one to fit in a special place or it can be an older building converted to take the small flock of birds. Some very nice small aviaries can be made on balconies and terraces as well as on the end of glass houses. Here again, overcrowding should be avoided so that the birds have plenty of free flying space without getting on top of each other, which only leads to squabbling. It is possible to buy ready-made, very decorative, small, flighted aviaries which are most suitable to put up in any garden. If the owner is handy with tools an aviary can soon be made, as the materials are easily obtainable.

As the aviary is outside, all food, water and grit vessels must be placed in the sleeping quarters so that they are

Aviary built on the end of an existing garden shed and (*right*) large open box cage on end of terrace wall. The tree affords natural shade.

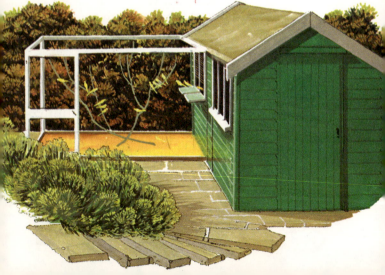

always in the dry. However, a special bathing place can be made so that the owner can watch the birds bathing and generally playing around on the ground. The perches can of course be plain wood but small branches from fruit trees are much more decorative and add to the appearance of the aviary. These perches can be renewed periodically so that the actual look of the aviary is changed somewhat.

The sleeping quarters and shelter should have a solid floor of either concrete or wood, and if wood, it should be raised from the ground so that any vermin attacks can be detected at once. Whether wood or concrete the floor will need covering with coarse, washed sand, or sand and sawdust, and again the internal perching should be fixed clear of the seed, water, and grit vessels.

If the owner has a small aviary of Canaries the odd mule or hybrid can be added for a little extra colouring. This will mean some slight adjustment to the seed mixture but all the birds will live quite happily together.

British birds — hardbills

Long before Canaries were known in Britain some of the native finch-like species were highly prized as singing pets. During the late Georgian and the Victorian periods Linnets and Goldfinches were favourite song birds in many small homes all over the country. Even today there are numerous people who prefer to have a British singing finch as a pet rather than a Canary.

It is now illegal for any unauthorized person to catch British birds and keep them caged. The vast majority are protected both during their breeding and non-breeding seasons and are not allowed to be offered for sale unless they are wearing the special closed metal rings, which indicate that they have been bred in captivity.

At the present time there are many strains of aviary and sometimes cage bred British birds. Their keen breeders take a great interest in maintaining and improving their various flocks of different species. It is mostly from these strains, which are in the process of being domesticated, that pet singing birds are obtained. As these birds will be wearing their breeder's special closed ring they can be sold freely if so desired.

Goldfinches, Greenfinches and Linnets all have their distinctive songs and individual ways and it is a matter of personal preference which species is selected for a family pet. Among the other varieties Bullfinches make most interesting pets, as although their own natural song is not especially attractive, they can be taught to pipe other tunes. At one time trained piping Bullfinches were exported from Europe and were sold in fair numbers, but nowadays such birds seem to have lost popularity as pets. It may be the fact that there are not sufficient people with an interest in training such birds, that tends to make them scarce.

Linnet (*Carduelis cannabina*), 5¼ins, in an old-fashioned cage in a cottage window (*left*). (*Below*) Victorian family watching a piping Bullfinch (*Pyrrhula pyrrhula*), 5¾ ins

Another species at one time trained to do tricks, was the Redpoll. These birds could be taught to fill their own seed or water pots by the means of a tiny bucket and pulley. It was really amazing how adept some birds became, using both their feet and beaks, to perform the operation of hauling a small bucket up some 12 to 16 inches. In addition to their skill in this respect, Redpolls have quite a nice, pleasing, soft song and become very friendly with their owners. There are, of course, other performing birds and the Japanese have trained some of their native tits to do similar tricks with buckets and pulleys.

Each year, birds belonging to a wide range of species get injured in some way or other and are nursed back to health by kindly people in all walks of life. In addition, numerous young birds that fall from their nests or have had their nest destroyed by some means are looked after and reared to maturity by interested people.

When birds from this category are well able to fend for themselves, they have frequently become so attached to the people that

Redpoll (*Carduelis flammea*), 4¾ ins

38

Many birds get injured through accidents or by fighting. Young birds are more prone to disasters and the young thrush (*right*) will have to be carefully cleaned and cared for if it is not to die from paint poisoning.

have saved them, that they refuse to leave the home when given the opportunity. Most of these birds are more suitable as outside pets, and will be discussed in a later chapter.

Green foodstuff is an essential part of the diet of hardbilled birds. If seeding plants and grasses are not available, then soaked seeds can become a substitute for the fresh wild seeds. The seed should be allowed to soak for several days so it begins to germinate, thus resembling the immature seed eaten by birds in the wild. Birds should also be provided with a good mineral mixture and this can be fed to the birds in a container that also contains sea sand and a calcium source, often crushed egg-shell.

If a group of finches are kept in a suitable aviary, or even if a pair are kept in a large cage, then it is quite possible that they will make a nest, even though no eggs may be laid. If the birds do seem to want to nest, then suitable material such as straw, moss and wool should be provided. The structures they make are frequently very attractive.

39

British birds – softbills

Generally speaking, as soon as most species of the smaller British softbilled birds have become accustomed to captivity, they will become exceedingly tame and very attached to their owners. It is very probable that many more people would keep softbills if it were not for the extra trouble that is needed to feed them and keep them clean and healthy.

It is well known that the range and variation of the Blackbird's and thrush's songs equals, and in many cases surpasses, those of the more exotic, imported, singing softbills. The few examples of these British species that are kept as household pets have endeared themselves to their owners through their confiding ways and beautiful song. The Mistle Thrush also has a clear and loud song but it lacks the variety and fullness of that of the Song Thrush.

Some Blackbirds and thrushes find their place as pets by being discovered as lost or deserted baby birds, and they have to be reared by hand. In doing so, the rearer appears to the birds as a rescuer and a parent and the birds usually

Large outdoor flight incorporating berry-bearing plants suitable for softbills. The birds (*left to right*) are: Mistle Thrush (*Turdus viscivorous*), 10½ ins; Song Thrush (*Turdus philomelos*), 9 ins; Blackbird (*Turdus merula*), 10 ins and Blackbird hen. A hen Blackbird feeds from its owner's hand.

become exceedingly attached to them.

Readers will realize that softbills are not suitable for housing in the same kind of all-wire decorative cages as are the hardbill varieties. The type of food that they must be given to eat often results in a nasty mess on the floor and walls of the cage. Softbills will live happily in box-type cages of some 3 feet in length and 18 inches high and wide. Such cages should be fitted with a loose sliding bottom which should be covered with blotting paper or some other absorbent material which will need changing daily to keep the cage sweet and fresh smelling. Access should be available to all parts of the cage so that it can be cleaned easily whenever necessary.

Their foods consist of a standard insectivorous soft food mixture prepared as directed on the container and can be bought at all bird accessory stores. Various soft fruits and a few live insects will complete their diet. Mealworms, which can be bought at pet shops, are often offered instead of other insects. On a dry weight basis they contain about 50% protein and 36% fat and are beneficial to most birds. They will also need plenty of fresh water for drinking purposes and should be allowed regular bathing facilities. This is very important with softbilled kinds, because the food they eat often causes their feathers to become somewhat soiled. Providing that the birds are healthy they can bath at all times of the year with no harmful results.

There are several strains of both Blackbirds and Song Thrushes that are breeding regularly in garden aviaries; some of these strains have been reproducing for many generations and, in addition, there are some unusual colour phases, mutations of the normal form, which are also breeding freely in captivity. Amongst these are the White, Pied

An unusual pet – a pied Blackbird cock. (*Right*) a suitable cage for softbills with a moveable base tray incorporating absorbent sheeting

and Dilute forms of Blackbirds and the Pied, Cinnamon and Dilute forms of the Song Thrushes.

The outdoor aviaries in which Blackbirds and thrushes are usually kept can be made most attractive by the planting of small trees, flowering bushes and shrubs, flowering plants and ornamental grasses. Ornamental shallow bathing places, old moss-covered logs and masonry can be arranged by the owner to give a most pleasing and colourful overall look. In addition to being nice to look at, the birds themselves get great delight in searching for various insects amongst the growing plants and other structures. With a little patience it is possible to get the birds of the aviary to come on the hand and to take tit-bits, quite fearlessly, from the owner's fingers.

There are odd specimens of nearly all softbilled birds that have, from time to time, become tame household pets. One day the reader may also have the opportunity of possessing one of these unusual and fascinating birds as a pet. If this does happen it is best to contact an experienced Bird Fancier for guidance on the feeding and general management of the pet. It should be noted that the majority of the hardbills live for many years in captivity but most of the softbills seem to have an even longer span.

Budgerigars

As there is a separate book in this series that deals exclusively with all aspects of the fascinating and colourful little Budgerigars, we will now only briefly discuss their housing, feeding and general management in the following paragraphs.

It can safely be said that Budgerigars as pet birds have given more comfort, pleasure and companionship to more people than any other bird known. Budgerigars have so much to recommend them as household pets; they are colourful, are simple to feed, become exceedingly tame and friendly, and above all they can be taught to imitate the human voice and other sounds. It is not to be wondered that these little birds are so popular as household pets in practically every country of the world.

Despite their undoubted popularity Budgerigars have only been kept in captivity for a little over 130 years. The numerous coloured varieties today are related to the wild Budgerigar of Australia, *Melopsittacus undulatus*. The wild bird is about 8 inches long with a tapering pointed tail. Usually it is grass-green with bright yellow on the head and a blue tail. There is much sooty scalloping and barring on the upper

Various coloured Budgerigars: (*from left to right*) Cobalt, Cinnamon Grey Blue, Pied Light Green, Opaline Violet Cobalt, Greywing Sky Blue

parts, with a royal blue patch on the cheek and three black spots on each side of the throat. As with the majority of wild birds that breed freely in captivity, mutations of colour occur. These mutations are purely a natural phenomenon and cannot be ascribed to changes in living conditions, although breeders are able to take a hand in the development of new strains by exploiting this variability.

Budgerigars are now bred in a wide selection of colours, ranging from the original light grass-green to olive green, yellow, blue, white, mauve, violet and composite colourings to mention just a few. This gives the intending owner of a pet Budgerigar a very big choice of shades and everyone can find a special colour to suit his own particular taste if he wishes. However, the colour of the pet bird has no bearing whatsoever on its ability to talk and become tame. This is the prerogative of individual birds of all colours over which we humans have no control, although we can help by careful handling of the new trainee.

Although both sexes of Budgerigars can become finger tame and learn to talk, it will usually be found that cock birds make the most successful pupils for training. Many hen birds, on the other hand, will get extremely tame and friendly with their owners and a few become really first-rate talkers. In any case it is always best to get a young bird straight from its parents, as soon as it can feed on its own, to train as a tame talking pet.

Many breeders, even experienced ones, find it difficult to be one hundred per cent sure of recognizing cock birds at this very early age. There are certain features that help in the

Young cock and hen Budgerigars in the nesting box. The cock is in the foreground.

choice of young cock birds, however. The ceres of the young cocks are a more purplish blue and bolder than those of the young hens, which are more inclined to be of a whitish shade and flatter in shape. Young cock birds are also generally quieter than hens and are less likely to bite, when first handled. Although this biting is not a sure sign it is one that does help in numerous cases. When fully adult the ceres of

In the above sex-linked crossing a Green hen is paired to a Lutino cock. The offspring will all be Lutino hens and Green cocks.

cocks become bright deep blue or purplish coloured and those of the hens are pale buff to deep chocolate brown. The cere is the small area just above the upper part of the beak where the nostril holes are situated and which is quite devoid of feathers.

Fanciers who breed birds specially for sale as talking pets make special pairings, so that they are certain of the sex of the young by their visual colouring. Such pairings are known as the sex-linked crosses, and a popular one in the Green kinds is Lutino cock to Green hen and in the Blue kinds Albino cock to Blue hen. In both of these pairings all the young cock birds are either green or blue coloured and all the young hens are red-eyed Lutinos or Albinos. From these pairings the young cocks can be recognized as soon as they hatch because they have black coloured eyes whereas all the hens will have definite red eyes.

Before the pet bird is actually bought, its new home must be considered and obtained. Because Budgerigars are so popular as household pets, it is quite easy to get really suitable cages from all good pet shops. These stores usually have a fine selection of decorative all-wire, wire and plastic and all-plastic cages to offer.

The cage selected can be made of any of these materials and it should be roomy, the materials of good quality, easy to clean, provided with seed, water and grit vessels and three perches. To facilitate cleaning, the cage should be fitted with a removable tray at the bottom, which can be covered with bird sand or a special sanded paper tray cover.

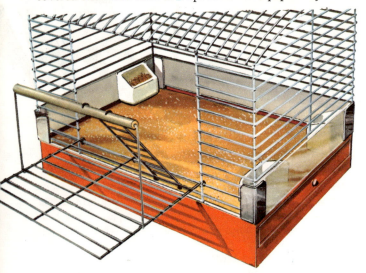

Budgerigars are very partial to toys and a great many different kinds can be found on sale. However, the number of toys given to any pet bird at one time should be strictly limited, so as not to cramp its cage space. If given too many toys a bird may also devote too much attention to them in preference to its owner, which of course is quite contrary to what is desired. A mirror hung in the cage is the best kind of cage toy and always appreciated by a bird. Small bells of different kinds, ladders of various lengths, and plastic balls of various sizes are all useful toys giving the pet both amusement and exercise.

As a pet bird often spends a considerable part of its time outside its cage, easy access in and out of the cage door is necessary. Small plastic platforms in a range of colours are to be had, and a platform of this kind or a perch attached near the door is really essential for every cage where the inmate is allowed to fly freely. Many birds become unsettled because they cannot get into the cage easily and the owner

The cage (*left*) has a well-fixed outside perch so that the bird can return easily. (*Below*) various Budgerigar toys

often has to catch the bird to put it back.

Budgerigars are very easy birds to feed and their needs to keep them fit and healthy are simple. Their diet consists of a mixture of canary seeds and millet seeds with millet sprays and green food. There are many very well-balanced, packeted Budgerigar seed mixtures on the market, all of which can be used with confidence. Millet sprays can usually be obtained in small plastic bags containing two or three sprays, or can be bought singly from bunches.

In addition to the foods mentioned above it is important that the birds have plenty of grit, cuttlefish bone and mineral nibbles at all times. This is essential whether they are kept in aviaries, flights, pens or cages. The grit is necessary for the proper assimilation of their food and the other materials contain various minerals and trace elements that are needed for their well-being.

When the cage has been bought and everything prepared for the reception of a new pet the bird itself can be obtained and installed. To be sure that a satisfactory bird is being bought it is best to order the bird well before the actual date required. If the bird is booked in good time it gives the seller time to select a bird of the right colour and sex required, which is more satisfactory to all concerned.

The first twenty-four hours or so in its new home are the most important time in a Budgerigar's life. The bird's success or failure as a tame pet is often governed by this period. If the following programme is carefully adhered to, the initial steps to the success of a tame, talking, pet Budgerigar are achieved.

When the new young Budgerigar is first taken home it should be gently released into its cage that contains the necessary food and water, and placed in a room and left quietly on its own until the following morning. This will give the bird an opportunity of quietly exploring the cage

and getting the feel of its new home without being disturbed. On the following morning one member of the family should go and see the bird to replenish the seed pot and change the water. While this is being done the bird's selected name should be clearly repeated a number of times. The name chosen should be a simple one of not more than two syllables. Every care must be taken not to frighten the bird in any way particularly during the first few weeks.

As previously stated the ability to talk will vary with each individual bird and this is a fact that must always be remembered. With some specimens the power of mimicry is very great indeed and the number of words and sentences learned can be quite surprising. However, if the owner does not talk slowly and clearly to the pupil, the bird's vocabulary can become a meaningless jumble of mixed words.

(*Left*) Cuttlefish and mineral nibbles that can be attached to the side of the cage. (*Right*) the owner's finger becomes a perch so that the Budgerigar can alight near its cage.

Although some birds do not seem to have much of a capacity to learn to repeat the human voice they will become astonishingly tame and will learn to perform many tricks. Some of these tricks may well be of their own invention and these can be developed and perfected by careful training. Here again, patience on the part of the owner when training a bird is most important if success is to be achieved.

Some pet Budgerigars will sleep peacefully on their owner's hand or shoulder when it is convenient. It is often found that pet birds become passionately fond of any kind of music and spend a lot of time listening to the radio and television.

A favourite pastime of many tame pet Budgerigars of both sexes is to bath under a dripping water tap in the kitchen sink. I know of several birds that fly right through the house to get their daily splash in the kitchen sink much to their owners' enjoyment. When a bird does this, or even when the bird is only allowed the freedom of one particular room, the owner must take special precautions to see that all doors and windows are securely fastened to prevent escape.

After having had a single tame pet Budgerigar for a time some people feel they would like to have more birds, even though they realize they would not be talkers. In such cases, unless the owner wishes to breed, it is best to have a small collection consisting of cock birds of mixed colours. By doing this the possibilities of fighting are reduced to a minimum and the birds themselves become much tamer and more friendly with their owner. A great deal of fun can be had from a small collection of various coloured cock birds housed in a small aviary on a terrace, a verandah, conservatory or summerhouse. Many times have I seen an owner walk into his aviary carrying a bunch of green food and within seconds all the birds are sitting on his hands and arms eating the green.

Sometimes when surroundings and conditions are suitable, a few people get the urge to keep Budgerigars at liberty in their gardens. This method of keeping Budgerigars, together with the actual breeding of them in cages, pens or aviaries, is fully explained in a companion book on Budgerigars.

Cut-away drawing of garden shed conversion to a small aviary. It consists of inside and outside flight for about twenty-four cock birds. The floor outside is cement with gravel chippings, inside there is a spare cage on a work-bench. All this still leaves enough space for garden tools.

Meyer's Parrot (*Poeocephalus meyeri*), from Equatorial Africa, total length 9 ins

FOREIGN BIRDS – PARROT-LIKE SPECIES

In the previous paragraphs the universally popular Budgerigars have been examined. These are just one of the parrot-like species, and we will now deal with some of the other varieties that are kept in captivity as household pets. For the sake of easy discussion, the parrot-like species can be roughly divided into groups each embracing birds with special characteristics – they are the parrots, macaws, cockatoos, parakeets and other varieties.

Parrots

True parrots, whatever their size or colour may be, have in common the special characteristic of a short tail. It can be safely said that a tame, talking parrot of any kind is a very attractive pet to have and can give its owner many years of pleasure and companionship. A great point in favour of the parrot tribe in general is the long life that these birds usually enjoy and in some cases parrots have been handed down for several generations within a family.

The most widely kept species of medium-sized parrots is the African Grey, undoubtedly achieving this position because of its great gift of mimicry. They do not have such vivid colouring in their plumage as some of their kindred species, being mainly silver grey with a bright red tail, but this is offset by their gentle behaviour and great talking ability.

Once an African Grey Parrot has established itself in a household and at least one member of the family has gained the bird's complete confidence, it is possible to allow a certain amount of time outside the cage, under supervision of course. As soon as an African Grey has been fully trained it can become really playful when at liberty; this applies equally to both cock and hen birds and the antics performed can delight the owner and friends for many hours on end. The tameness which some specimens attain is really surprising and their behaviour can be likened to a pet dog. In fact there are many instances where owners have dogs, which form lasting friendships with parrots. As the actual feeding and training of all parrots are similar, these will be discussed together later on in this chapter.

African Grey Parrot (*Psittacus erithacus*), from Equatorial Africa, about 13 ins

One of the most popular parrots that also comes from Africa is the delightful little Senegal Parrot which is only some 9 inches in overall length. In colouring, the Senegals are quite pleasing, being a mixture of soft greys, greens and bright orange-yellow, which makes a delightful contrast of colour shades.

When first imported, Senegals must be treated a little carefully and not subjected to cold or dampness for the first few weeks. Once they have become fully acclimatized they are very tough little creatures and can stand cold winters even in an outdoor aviary without any heat.

Because they are small and very friendly by nature, some owners keep two in the same cage. They usually become attached to their owner as well as to each other and are one of the few parrots that can actually be kept in pairs as household pets. Although not anywhere near as talkative as the African Grey they will say some words or sentences.

Senegal Parrot (*Poeocephalus senegalus*), Gambia, just over 9 ins. (*Opposite*) Yellow-naped Amazon Parrot (*Amazona auropalliata*), western Mexico, 14 ins

The group of parrots which are most widely kept and in great variety are those which come from South America and are known as the Amazon group. Of these only a limited number of varieties are freely imported and kept as tame, talking, household pets. They vary a great deal in size and are mainly green in colour, with various areas of blue, orange and red making the difference in the varieties. Three popular kinds are the Blue-fronted, Yellow-headed and Yellow-fronted Amazons, all of which, if taken young, can be trained as talkers, most of them becoming quite fluent. Temperament varies with individual birds but as a whole they are of a kindly nature and will become extremely friendly towards their owner and other members of a family.

It is not necessary to enlarge further on all the varieties of parrots that are occasionally kept as household pets. They all need the same kind of treatment as the birds that have been mentioned so far.

The main diet of parrots is a mixture of large canary seed, sunflower with a little hemp, oats, dari, maize, and various soft fruits and nuts, including ground-nuts. Some birds like certain root vegetables such as carrot, parsnip, celery heart or even artichokes. It is necessary that they all get a reasonable amount of fruit and vegetables to keep them in a fit and healthy condition.

(*Above and below*) two types of parrot cage that can be used to keep these birds in the house. Care should be taken to see that the bird's tail does not catch on the bars.

All animal fats, sweet cakes or biscuits containing sugar should be strictly avoided as these will only make the birds overweight and lazy and can also cause overheating of the blood which may lead to the horrible habit of self-feather-plucking. The birds need a regular supply of grit, fresh, clean water, and something hard like old mortar, cuttlefish bone, or a mineral block to nibble, so that their beaks are kept at a reasonable length. They will also like, periodically, pieces of

The basic foodstuffs for parrots consists of large seeds, nuts and soft fruits.

fruit-tree branches to gnaw and any of the wood and bark they may eat is beneficial and at the same time good for their beaks.

Most parrots are kept in either round or square, all-metal cages, made of stout material because of their powerful beaks. As large a cage as possible should be bought for a parrot and the extra expense is adequately compensated for by the bird's better health and condition. The most important thing with a caged parrot, however, is to let it out of the cage regularly, preferably every day.

Some parrots will like to have a bath in a shallow dish or even hung out in their cage for a time in a warm shower of rain. Since this means drying the cage thoroughly afterwards, however, many owners prefer to spray the birds regularly with a fine warm spray of rainwater. The owner will in course of time discover how the individual parrot reacts to a particular form of management, and as already stated, they are all individuals and, thus, behaviour varies considerably.

Some birds also like root vegetables and celery and cuttlefish bone is good for their beaks.

Blue and Yellow Macaw (*Ara ararauna*),
tropical America, 31 ins. This is one of the
best talking macaws and the coloration is
superb. They are extremely hardy birds and
will even nest under suitable conditions.

Macaws

Some people like to have rather spectacular birds as pets and
of the parrot-like species the macaws fill this need admirably.
The majority of macaws kept as individual pets are massive
birds, up to 3 feet in overall length and with tremendously
powerful beaks. Their colourings are very vivid blues,
yellows, reds and golds making very showy combinations.

Although macaws have such powerful beaks, which in the
wild state they use to open the hard nuts which form the
main part of their diet, they are extremely gentle with their
owners. They can be fed chiefly on monkey-nuts and sunflower seeds and a small amount of oats, maize, and canary
seed can be added. Fruit, such as apple, should be given
regularly.

No ordinary parrot cage is large enough to house the
largest, and most familiar, of these birds and macaws are
usually kept on T-shaped stands, fixed to this by means of
a light, strong, steel chain attached to a leg. The birds do
not seem to mind this method of tethering and live quite
happily under such circumstances. By being chained to a

stand they can exercise their long wings quite freely and their long tail is free to move unhindered by cage bars.

The plumage of a macaw will, like the parrots, suffer if the bird does not get a bath of some kind. Since these birds are generally kept on a stand it is a simple procedure, in warm weather, to put the bird outside in a light shower of rain. If this is not possible they can be periodically sprayed with rain water. Basically the treatment is the same as parrots.

The most well-known of the macaws are the Red and Yellow and the Blue and Yellow Macaws. These are frequently seen on their T-shaped stands at zoos. The popularity of the macaws in general, relies on their superb coloration and the ease with which they can be kept. Some individual birds will make good talkers, but their natural voice is a screech that is loud and raucous.

(*Top*) the Hyacinthine Macaw (*Anodorhyncus hyacinthinus*), central Brazil, 34 ins. The beak of this species appears formidable but it is actually particularly gentle. (*Left*) a Red and Yellow Macaw (*Ara macao*), Mexico and Central America, 36 ins, probably the most well-known of the macaws.

The Roseate Cockatoo (*Eolophus roseicapillus*), Australia, just over 14 ins. It is often known as the Rose-breasted Cockatoo or Galah.

Cockatoos

Cockatoos provide us with many amusing household pets, and although some of them are inclined to be a little boisterous and noisy, they nevertheless can be really fascinating in their funny ways. Their general colour is white with the pink, or yellow, tinted crest, which they will raise when they are excited, displaying a blaze of colour on their otherwise white plumage. The talking ability of the cockatoo group varies quite a lot. Many of them will become exceedingly tame and yet only repeat the odd word or two, whereas others are extremely talkative, as well as being tame and friendly with their owners.

There seems to be something especially attractive about cockatoos and this will be noticed at all zoos, and in fact, at any place where a number of parrot-like birds are housed together. Generally they are kept under the same conditions

Great Black Cockatoo (*Microglossus aterrimus*), Australia and New Guinea, 30 ins (*left*). Also known as the Palm Cockatoo. (*Right*) the Greater Sulphur-crested Cockatoo (*Kakatoe galerita*), Australia, 20 ins

as parrots, that is in stout all-wire cages. Sometimes one of the larger species will be kept on a T-shaped stand like a macaw and it seems to suit them very well indeed. Caged birds should be let out frequently and also given plenty of things to do to amuse them. If it is given an empty cotton reel to play with it will also help the bird to exercise its beak.

Perhaps the most frequently kept of the smaller cockatoos is the Roseate, or Rose-breasted, Cockatoo, or Galah, as it is mostly called in its native Australia. These are quite small birds but of lovely colouring. They will become very friendly and tame but are not good at repeating the human voice.

Cockatoos of all varieties need the same kind of seed as true parrots, together with nuts, fruits and root vegetables. Some birds are extremely fond of garden peas and broad-beans, but the quantities given should of course be controlled, as all foods other than the standard seed mixtures.

63

Parakeets

The number of beautifully coloured parakeets coming from many parts of the world is very large, and they are sometimes kept as household pets. Of these the Ring-necks, which exist in a number of varieties, are the most popular and most probably some of the oldest parrot-like birds to be kept as pets by human beings. Although a few female Ring-necks have been kept as single pets, it is generally understood that the male birds are much more suitable as pets and are less likely to be spiteful to their owners. Ring-necks and other parakeets are usually kept in the typical, all-wire parrot cage, which seems to suit them very well indeed. It is not possible in a book of this nature to explain all the different and beautifully coloured parakeets that do exist and could possibly be kept as pets, but it is possible to name in addition to the popular Ring-neck family, a few of the more common household pets. One of the most popular is the Cockatiel (*Nymphicus hollandicus*), a small Australian parakeet of some

Plum-headed Parakeet (*Psittacula cyano-cephala*), India and Ceylon, 14 ins

Crimson-winged Parakeet (*Atros mictus*), Australia and New Guinea, 12 ins

13 inches long, that has the additional attraction of having an upright crest on its head. Cockatiels are very gentle by nature and can be trained to become tame quite easily. With a little perseverance on the part of the owner most of the single, tame birds will learn to repeat words and even sentences, which all adds to their attraction. Pairs of Cockatiels often become quite inseparable.

Some of the South American parakeets known as Conures (*Aratinga* species) make very good single pets and particularly so the Nandy, Quaker and Golden-crowned kinds. Another very popular South American parakeet is the Orange-chinned Parakeet or Tovi (*Brotogeris jungularis*), which ranges north to Mexico and is about 7 inches in length. It is frequently called the Bee Bee in America. These latter have a particular aptitude for becoming a tame and friendly companion to their owner, even though their talking ability is very small indeed. A near relation is the Tui Parakeet which is smaller but has the same temperament.

Rock Pebbler Parakeet (*Polytelis anthopeplus*), Australia, 16 ins

Blue-, or Slaty-headed Parakeet (*Psittacula himalayana*), India to Indo-China, 14 ins

All the parakeets feed on a mixture of canary seed and millet seed to which some sunflower, hemp, oats and dari have been added. Fortunately, nowadays, good packeted seeds suitable for all kinds of parrot-like birds can be obtained from pet shops. Green foods of various kinds and some sweet fruits should also form part of the diet for parakeets. Most of the varieties are extremely fond of seeding grasses and chickweed, and many will eat the stalky heart of lettuce and cabbage when other green foods are not readily available. Mixed grits must always be supplied and these are essential for the well-being of the birds. Pieces of cuttlefish bone should also be given and pieces from branches of fruit trees help to exercise the birds' beaks and keep them in a good healthy condition. It is usual to supply parakeets with a large flat vessel of water for bathing and occasionally a fine spray will be appreciated by the birds.

The larger parakeets can well be housed in the smaller kind of all-wire parrot cages and such cages do not need any adapting for parakeets. The smaller kinds can be housed in the large fancy wire cages as sometimes used for pet Budgerigars. Many of these cages are quite roomy and most suitable for this purpose.

Many-coloured Parakeet (*Psephotus varius*), Australia, 11½ ins, being sprayed, with a fine hand spray

Masked Lovebirds (*Agapornis
personata*), from East Africa,
6 ins

Lovebirds

Another kind of parrot-like bird is the lovebird, which may
be kept either singly or in pairs, although of course single
birds do actually make the most suitable pets. It must be
pointed out here lovebirds are not Budgerigars, although
Budgerigars are sometimes called 'Lovebirds' because of their
friendly nature. Lovebirds are true, short-tailed parrots
whereas Budgerigars are parakeets with long tapering tails.

There are several species of lovebirds with a main bright
green colouring and some yellow, black or red markings on
their heads and throats. The Masked Lovebird is the form
most commonly bred in captivity and the Rosy-faced
Lovebird is another attractive and slightly larger species
that is also quite popular. Some lovebirds, particularly those
when taken young, will learn to say a few words and their
voices are quite clear and distinct, in spite of the small size
of the birds.

The lovebirds, either singly or in pairs, can be housed in
Budgerigar-type, all-metal cages and need the same kind of
feeding and general management as the smaller parakeets
that have just been mentioned.

Lorikeets

A further kind, and quite a different one, is the lorikeet group, comprising a considerable number of extremely beautiful, highly-coloured birds, which quickly become tame and friendly with their owner. However, there is one big drawback with keeping these birds, as they are nectar and fruit-eating birds, and have to be kept under much more hygienic conditions.

If the owner has suitable accommodation, for instance a summer house or verandah, then one of these gaily coloured birds makes an ideal friendly companion. One particular variety, the Blue Mountain Lorikeet, is an extremely tame one and even in the wild can be encouraged to come down and feed from the hands of visitors. There are several parks in Australia, their native country, where flocks of these rainbow-hued birds descend on visitors to take tit-bits from their hands.

Pet lorikeets, however, will require a cage with a suitable bottom, in order that it can be covered with absorbent material for easy and constant cleaning. The majority of owners seem to favour using

Blue Mountain Lorikeets (*Trichoglossus haenatodus*), feeding from the hands of visiting Australians. They are also known as Swainson's, or Rainbow, Lorikeets and come from Australasia, measuring about 12½ inches in length.

blotting paper or a similar absorbent paper. Their food consists of soft, ripe, fresh fruit, sometimes difficult to obtain, and a nectar which can be made up of honey or baby food, diluted with water. Special containers for this type of food are obtainable at good pet shops. Because of the nature of their food these birds do not need to eat grit or cuttlefish bone as do the other species of parrot-like birds, they do, however, appreciate pieces of fruit-tree branches to nibble and this will help exercise their beaks.

There is of course a wide range of other parrot-like birds, which occasionally are taken as pets and they range from the tiny parrotlets to the huge Black Cockatoos. However, the feeding and management of the different species mentioned in the foregoing paragraphs will cover any of these birds should the need arise.

FOREIGN BIRDS – HARDBILLS

The parrot-like species of foreign birds only comprise a small part of the foreign birds that are kept as pets. A great proportion of the foreign, seed-eating birds are kept for decorative purposes and usually in several pairs together, either in an indoor aviary or a large, planted, garden aviary according to taste and space available. Many of these species become quite tame and will take food from the hands of their owners but, of course, they do not have the appeal of parrot-like birds. Some species are not only colourful but also have a sweet song and are kept as pets for this purpose alone. Of the singing birds, perhaps the cardinals and singing finches are the most popular and easy to obtain. Most finches are colourful, easy to keep and generally obtainable from all good pet shops.

For small indoor collections the tiny waxbills and their related species can make up charming little collections, and

1. The Parson Finch (*Poephila cincta*), Australia, 4½ ins
2-8. Varieties of waxbill:
2. Red-eared, or Common, Waxbill (*Estrilda troglodytes*), Central Africa, 3½-4 ins
3. Golden-breasted (*Estrilda subflavia*), West Africa, 3¼-3½ ins
4. Yellow-bellied (*Estrilda melanotis quartinia*), western Africa, 3¾ ins
5. Orange-cheeked (*Estrilda melpoda*), West Africa, 4 ins

6. Crimson-rumped (*Estrilda rhodopyga*), East Africa, 4½ ins
7. St Helena (*Estrilda astrild*), Central Africa, 4-4½ ins
8. Black-cheeked (*Estrilda erythronotos*), south-western Africa, about 4½ ins

some of them have quite sweet, though somewhat limited songs. The smallest of this group are the minute Golden-breasted Waxbills which are just short of 3½ inches long. The St Helena Waxbills are a larger species, which are beautifully marked with fine grey undulating lines on a grey background. The underparts are washed with a deep pink that deepens to red and a brilliant red eye-streak. They have a long tail which is flitted fanwise when they are excited. The Red-eared Waxbills have a similar coloration which is mainly a soft grey. The lower breast is washed with a pale pink colour and there is a narrow patch of red near each ear; from which the bird gets its name. These are inexpensive birds to buy from pet shops and are hardy and easy to handle.

Virginian Cardinal (*Richmondena cardinalis*), comes from the United States and measures 8-9 ins. It is also known as the Scarlet Cardinal or Virginian Nightingale.

The cardinals are quite large birds similar in size to the Song Thrush, and of these the Virginian and Red Crested Cardinals are the most popular. Both kinds of birds are long lived and have a sweet song and, of course, are very easy to feed. One of the easiest species to keep is the Green Cardinal (*Gubernatrix cristata*), which breeds easily and is hardy enough to winter outside in a flight if necessary. It is not, unfortunately, as colourful as the Red-crested species and is slightly more difficult to obtain therefore.

Being large birds cardinals will naturally require a reasonably large cage and most people keep such birds in box-type cages. These are made of light wood and have a strong wire front, and naturally can be decorated to suit the surrounding room. Their food consists of millet seed, canary seed, a little hemp seed, and soft fruit, together with the usual grit, cuttlefish bone and green food.

The singing finch-type of birds are quite small and can be housed in the usual, all-wire, canary cage. Their food is similar to that of the canary, being mainly canary seed, small millet seed and millet sprays. Many of these little birds live for a very long time in these conditions and some Green Singing Finches have lived up to 25 years with the cock bird still singing. Long life in small birds of any kind, however, is the exception rather than the rule.

Waxbills and similar types of small foreign birds can be kept in small indoor aviaries and, if so, they will need these structures made with small mesh, wire netting, although the actual shape of the cages can be arranged to fit in to any particular given spot. Here again the owner's decorative ability can come into play and very pleasing structures, can be had. These can be filled with various species of hardbilled birds and, since there is a very wide scope of choice for size, colour and shape, most interesting and fascinating collections can be built up. Only a few of the very large number of possible birds have been named here and it is up to the prospective owner to choose the types required by visiting other fanciers or the local pet stores.

The wide box-type cage (*below*) is suitable for the Virginian Cardinal. It measures 3 ft in length and has a piece of decorative tree bark inside. It is painted to complement the colour of the bird.

FOREIGN BIRDS – SOFTBILLS

Here again, there is a wide range of different, softbilled, foreign birds that are periodically imported and even bred by keen aviculturists. Many of the species are highly coloured and some have a beautiful song, which of course recommends them as pets. But again their feeding makes it a little more difficult.

For many centuries various softbilled birds have been kept as pets in Near and Far Eastern countries. In Persia and the surrounding countries the Bulbuls are favourite song birds, and the singing tone of some of them is exceedingly sweet and can be compared favourably with the Nightingale. In the ancient Chinese empires singing softbills were well known and are depicted on their silk paintings, their porcelain, or carved in precious metals and stones. In fact it can safely be said that the keeping of species of softbilled birds is even more popular throughout the world than that of the hardbilled kinds.

Modern travel and scientific knowledge have made it possible for the gorgeous and minute hummingbirds to be transported all over the world and they actually live most successfully in captivity. These are the smallest birds known and in flight they resemble large dragonflies. In captivity they must be fed nectar which they take on the wing from special containers. Only the most experienced bird fanciers are able to supply conditions suitable for these birds and a visit to a large zoo will show the reader how these minute creatures are kept in a happy, healthy condition.

The most popular singing pet softbills seem to be the Shama, Pekin Robin and the Bulbuls, and the Shama (*Cittocincla macrura*) is generally thought to have the most glorious song of them all. This bird is long-lived and easy to keep very soon becoming tame enough to take food from its owner's hand. They are blue-black in colour with brown underparts. The tail is black with white at the base and tip. Shamas are about 11 inches in length and about half of this is taken up by the tail.

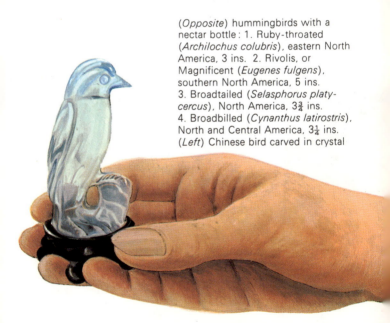

(*Opposite*) hummingbirds with a nectar bottle: 1. Ruby-throated (*Archilochus colubris*), eastern North America, 3 ins. 2. Rivolis, or Magnificent (*Eugenes fulgens*), southern North America, 5 ins. 3. Broadtailed (*Selasphorus platycercus*), North America, 3¾ ins. 4. Broadbilled (*Cynanthus latirostris*), North and Central America, 3¼ ins. (*Left*) Chinese bird carved in crystal

Bulbuls are also known as Persian Nightingales and many of the different kinds are frequently kept in highly ornamented cages as singing pets in large houses in the East. The Pekin Robin (*Liothrix luteus*) is known as the Pekin Nightingale and is one of the most frequently kept smaller foreign softbills, being attractive in colour with a sweet song.

All these species need cages of the box-type and of a similar size to that of the previously mentioned cardinals.

Red-vented Bulbul (*Pycnonotus cafer*), India, 8 ins. These birds tame quickly and their song is melodious, if monotonous. (*Left also*) some of the favourite foods of fruit-eating birds

It is essential in these cages to have a special bottom that can be easily removed, in order that absorbent paper or other material can be put on to the floor to absorb the moisture from the droppings.

These species need fresh fruit such as grapes, pears, bananas and oranges, and an insectivorous soft food to keep them fit and well. These insectivorous foods can be bought in packets, of different mixtures according to species, from good pet shops. It will be realized that with such a pet the cage must always be kept spotlessly clean, for the owner's sake if not for the bird!

All softbills, both large and small, are very keen on bathing and must be provided with the means for this. It is usually found most practical to give the bird a bath just before it is due to be cleaned out, so that the cage can be kept clean and dry. It is a matter of individual preference whether the bath used is one that is hung on the open door or one that is put inside the cage. The perches of all softbilled birds should be cleaned daily and it is probably best to keep spare sets of perches so that they can be changed quickly.

Greater Hill Mynah (*Gracula religiosa religiosa*), Indonesia, 10½-13 ins. Also known as the Javanese, or Northern, Hill Mynah

Mynahs

In recent years the most popular of all the softbills have been birds of the mynah family. This group of birds comes from India and the surrounding areas and belongs to the same family as the starlings. Mynahs have a special appeal to many pet bird-keepers since they can imitate the human voice and other sounds with great clarity. In addition, they become exceedingly tame and friendly with the owner and family and their wonderful talking ability makes them very attractive as household pets.

The Common Mynah (*Acridotheres tristis*) comes from India and is about 9½ inches in length. The head is black and the upper parts a brownish red with brown wings and a white-tipped tail. The brown eyes have a dark ring and the cere is yellow. These birds can be kept together with other larger birds or, if kept singly, will soon become completely tame. In comparison with other mynahs the colouring appears dull but the liveliness of the bird itself is adequate compensation.

Lesser Hill Mynah (*Gracula religiosa indica*), India, 10 ins. Also known as the Southern Hill Mynah

The most popular of the mynahs are the Greater and Lesser Hill Mynahs, which are birds of black plumage with strange, yellow-coloured skin appendages decorating their head and face. Although both these species are popular pets, the Lesser is more frequently seen. Although they sometimes scream their voice is not too unpleasant.

These birds are mostly taken from the nests when very young and reared by hand, and consequently they become quite fearless of human beings and do not object to being handled. It would seem that mynahs are very quick at learning to imitate the human voice, which they do very clearly and with the exact intonation of their teacher. Some pets are so good at imitating their owners voice that they can cause great confusion in a household. As with parrots, language is no barrier and they can learn to repeat words and sentences in any tongue. Mynahs that have been kept in close proximity to any engineering works, or factories, learn to imitate various mechanical sounds to perfection and it is often very difficult to tell the imitated noise from the real one.

Because of the nature of their food, which consists of an insectivorous mixture, both fresh and dried, biscuit meal, dried fruits and fresh soft fruits, they have to be housed in cages specially constructed for easy cleaning. For this purpose it is possible to get all-metal, box-type cages with the necessary feeding equipment attached. These cages are very easy to clean and the birds can be kept in a spotless condition. Some mynahs can be housed successfully in the large type of all-wire parrot cages but if so then the cage must be kept scrupulously clean, preferably with absorbent sheeting on the floor. Such cages are useful when a bird is allowed outside and can have a natural bath in the rain, which they seem to enjoy greatly and which keeps their plumage in good condition. Care should be taken afterwards, however, to see that the cage is thoroughly dried.

Their soft food, which should be of the coarse kind, can

be obtained from bird accessory stores and be mixed with dried fruits such as currants, raisins and sultanas. Some bird food manufacturing firms put up a special packet of soft food blended for mynahs and this saves owners the trouble of mixing their own. In addition to this they will appreciate a little live insect food in the form of maggots and meal worms, which again can be bought at the appropriate stores, and they can also be given finely chopped raw meat and hard-boiled eggs.

Although Mynahs will eat practically any kind of soft fruits, grapes and oranges seem to be the most favoured. Some owners add a little grated carrot with the insectivorous food and many birds seem to enjoy this addition. As with all birds, individuals have their own strange little fancies with regard to food and this can only be discovered by their owners in the course of time.

(*Top left*) a special type of cage that is suitable for a mynah with side pieces to catch thrown bits. (*Left from top to bottom*) selection of suitable foodstuffs: soft fruits, mealworms or chopped meat, biscuit meal and dried fruit.

The training of a young mynah should follow the procedure suggested for parrot-like birds set out earlier in this chapter. When a young mynah is obtained it will need special care and, if possible, should be fed on the same food that it was first reared on. This information can usually be obtained from the pet store when the bird is obtained. The change-over to the new, and what will become the standard diet, should be gradual so as not to upset the young bird's digestive system. It is important to note that this procedure is one that should be adopted with every kind of newly-imported bird whether young or old. If this is done it will very often save a bird from becoming unwell and also ensure that the change of habitat will be less upsetting for the pet.

As soon as the bird has completely settled down to its new surroundings its initiation to mimicry can be started. To ensure that the words and sentences are clearly repeated they should be of limited number and new ones should not be introduced until the first ones have been fully mastered. It is also best to leave the training to one person, in order not to confuse the bird with a mixture of voice tones. While care is taken over the training of a bird, the owner must also see that the pet gets enough exercise, either in a large enough cage or by flying freely. Otherwise it will easily grow fat and lazy and be a far less interesting pet.

A young Indian mynah being trained to talk. It is essential that only one person undertakes this task in the early stages so that the bird can become accustomed to their voice.

A mynah will often form a firm friendship with the household pet cat or dog and it can be most amusing to see a cat or dog come bounding into a room, after its name is called by the mynah using the exact intonation of its owner's voice. Many people are also very surprised when they hear their names spoken by a mynah, because of the amazing similarity to the voice of a human-being. It seems reasonable to say that a mynah will make the most attractive and amusing pet of all the non-parrot-like birds. The only drawback is that it is a softbilled bird.

The main species of birds that can really be described as true household pets have now been dealt with and now some of the other varieties of birds that can be kept as pets in other circumstances can be discussed.

OUTDOOR PET BIRDS

Doves and pigeons

Doves and pigeons are probably the most popular and widely-kept birds in the world. In actual fact they both belong to the same family of birds and the only reason for calling them by different names is their size; the smaller ones are usually doves and the larger types pigeons.

The keeping of any species of pigeon as a captive pet dates back a very long way into the histories of many countries and particularly those of the Near and Far East. For genera-

Fancy pigeons;
Oriental Frill,
Jacobin

tions, doves have been the symbol of peace and although many doves are peaceful as a species, some of them are quite vicious when they meet others at breeding times. Some of the earliest mentions of doves, familiar to most people, are in the Bible where they frequently appear as symbols of peace.

Of all the many pigeons, and there are some 300 species, the Rock Dove (*Columba livida*) is perhaps the most important. It is a native of southern Europe, north Africa and central and southern Asia. Artificial selection has given rise to many varieties differing in colour, size, shape, and voice.

Bald-headed Tumbler

Crested Mucky

With succeeding generations, however, even the most ornate birds will show an increasing resemblance to the Rock Dove. The flocks of pigeons that can be seen in many towns and cities today are domestic birds that have become wild.

The Pouter Pigeon is a popular breed. The bird is able to blow up its crop enormously and appears quite comical. The Oriental Frills are the most attractive birds of the Frill varieties and the Jacobins also have feather ruffs; in this case almost hiding the face.

The Racing Pigeon resembles the Rock Dove and is bred popularly for its homing instincts. These birds occur in many patterns and colour variations and can fly at speeds that can reach 50 to 55 miles per hour.

White doves are frequently used by conjurors and, when well-trained, can be used to perform remarkable tricks. They show up well against colourful backgrounds.

One of the most consistently popular pigeons is the Fantail with its magnificent tail. The Tumblers are also popular because of their flying prowess but their shape and colour varies. Other varieties include Homers, German Trumpeters, Carrier Pigeons and many types of dove. The Passenger Pigeon (*Ectopistes migratorius*), is a now extinct species that came from North America. They were slender birds with a long tail and last century existed in flocks of millions. Slaughter by man was the cause of their disappearance and the last one died in captivity in 1914.

Generally speaking, only a few of the many varieties such as Fantails, Pouters and Tumblers are kept as pets, either singly or in pairs in cages, or in large numbers in aviaries or cotes. With the doves it is generally the domesticated White and Barbary kinds that are kept as pets but examples of the many other species may sometimes be found as pets.

Because of their very placid ways doves are used by magicians and conjurors most satisfactorily and it would

Pigeons and doves are very suitable pets for children for they can live in many different situations, are easy to keep and tame and do not mind being handled.

appear that the birds seem to delight in their unusual work. They can also be trained to perform tricks and there are many troupes entertaining the public at the present time. It seems that once trained the birds have no fear whatsoever of lights, noises, or surroundings, and just go through their performance placidly.

Many people have their first introduction to a pet bird through having a dove or pigeon in their childhood. This is quite understandable as these birds are easy to handle, are strong and sturdy, are hardy, can be kept almost anywhere, and above all are simple to feed. It is possible to keep them in an ordinary good-sized cage but they should be allowed to fly freely as often as possible. When they are let out of their cage, doors and windows should be shut and, until they are used to one another, cats or dogs should be kept away. Pigeons and doves are very suitable for young people and, if kept singly, can become very attached to their owner and will follow him almost anywhere.

It is always best to obtain pet doves and pigeons when they are young birds and consequently much more easy to train. Most bird stores have supplies of young birds during the spring and summer months and, from them, the choice of species can be made. As with all other kinds of birds, the accommodation should be first arranged and then the bird, or birds, bought.

A structure to hold a single bird or a pair need not be very elaborate and can be sited indoors, in any outhouse, or on a verandah or terrace. If the birds are allowed to fly freely then the house in which they are kept should have the outside painted brightly or otherwise made conspicuous. The birds will then easily be able to find their way back there after flying out. All the birds basically require is a dry sleeping place and a place in which to fly. This, of course, gives the prospective owner ample scope to indulge in his or her own special ideas on housing. The food, water and grit vessels should be placed in the covered section and the floor covered with sand, fine gravel or peat moss.

If the house is large enough for the owner to walk inside, the bird or birds will soon become very tame and take food

Fantails with Beagle hounds. These attractive birds are usually kept for ornamental purposes but, nevertheless, make entertaining pets.

from the hand and after a time learn to sit on the hand or arm and be carried about. Of course, as with the training of any bird, gentleness must be the most important feature and sudden noises or movements must be avoided if the trainee is to become really tame.

It is possible to start with a few pairs of, for example, White Fantails in an enclosed bird house, and then when they are thoroughly tame they can be transferred to an outside dovecote. These birds can then enjoy full freedom and at the same time still retain their affection for their owner and come to hand for food, much to the enjoyment of the family and visitors. The domesticated doves can also be treated in the same manner but they usually take a little longer to settle down to these conditions, although when once really accustomed to the life they enjoy it to the full. Special care should be taken with the white breeds of doves, since they have a very trusting nature and are very conspicuous because of their coloration. Frequently they become easy prey for cats or owls and many owners prefer to house them in large outside wired flights where they will live perfectly happily providing they are not overcrowded.

As has already been stated doves and pigeons are very easy to feed, but seem to do best on a mixture of maple peas, small beans, wheat, barley and occasionally a few clipped oats. A little maize is also appreciated by most. Although they will eat many kinds of household scraps these should be avoided if the birds are to be kept in good, clean, hard feather. Like all seed-eating birds they must have grit and green food and it is especially important, where the birds are at liberty, that they have access to green food to prevent them straying into the vegetable or flower garden. Drinking water should be supplied in tall vessels but they should also be given flat shallow dishes for bathing purposes. The birds kept outside will, of course, always take advantage of rain showers, from which they will benefit and derive a lot of enjoyment.

During the course of each year a few young Turtle Doves (*Streptopelia turtur*) are found deserted by their parents and are reared by hand, but when the season for migrating comes along the birds seem to get a desire to go with their

The normal dovecote is barrel-shaped, positioned at the top of a pole, but many larger and more elaborate types can be made. (*Above*) Java Turtle Dove (*Streptopelia bitorquata*), East Indies and the Phillipines, 12 ins (*below*) Eastern Collared, or Collared Turtle, Dove (*Streptopelia decaocto*), Europe, 11 ins

flocks, and however tame they may be, take the first opportunity to fly away to distant lands. Similarly young Wood Pigeons or Ring Doves (*Columba palumbus*) are sometimes hand-reared and kept as pets but they can become such a nuisance in the garden that they have to be sent back to the woods.

Since the increased popularity of Eastern Collared Doves as a breeding species, numbers of young ones have also been hand-reared. They seem to make better pets than Turtle Doves as they are of a more placid nature. Another bird that is also increasing in popularity is the Diamond Dove (*Geopelia cuneata*). This bird comes from Australia and is also known as the Little Dove or Red-eyed Dove. The attractive, slender Mourning Dove (*Zenaidura macroura*), is a grey and brown species that is common in North and Central America.

It is of interest to note that many well-known aviculturists have started on their careers by first keeping pigeons or doves as youngsters. Later they then graduated to the keeping of many other species of birds that are domesticated today.

Poultry

A considerable number of ordinary domestic poultry find their way into private establishments as outside pet birds. Often a small or weakly chick in a brood invariably receives special care by the owner and often ends up as a family pet, making a strong vigorous one too. This is generally due to the bird becoming so very tame during the process of being reared, that it attaches itself to the owner rather than to its own mother. Cases of young birds and animals adopting the people who care for them as parents while they are very young, are quite frequent both with wild and domesticated kinds. Of course newly hatched chicks are most attractive little balls of fluff and just ask to be cared for by someone.

One case that can be cited as an example is of a Rhode Island Red hen that was hand reared from a few days old. When too big for the house she was banished to the stables. Although she was fed there, she would confidently come to the kitchen door and knock on it, expecting to gain admittance. She remained perfectly tame throughout her life, not only towards the owners but also towards the other pets in the family, and would feed on almost any scraps of food from anyone who cared to feed her. When she died at about ten years old she was sadly missed. Many other instances and diverse stories occur about pet hens and this is but one very typical example.

All varieties of domestic fowls and their very numerous crosses can be taken as pets and it will generally be found that hens are preferable to cocks, although with many other species it is mostly the cock birds that make the best family pets. The cock birds are quite attractive and friendly while young but, as they become fully adult, they are very inclined to become aggressive and even quite nasty with their owner. There are, of course, odd cases with certain breeds where a cockerel will always remain tame and attached to its owner.

(*Left*) a Leghorn cross hen with her chicks. (*Right*) decorative use of a bantam in a Japanese print

There are many different types of fowl but the ancestor of all domestic poultry is the Red Jungle Fowl (see page 9). In the wild state chickens live in woods, forest edges or very grassy fields. Variations of the species have been influenced chiefly by the climate and through selective breeding by man.

Domestication has produced three types of bird: fighting birds, food birds and show birds. Cock fighting takes place between birds that have been specially bred for their bravery and killing instincts. It is a horrible 'sport' that has been forbidden in many parts of the world, although it still does take place. People who have seen cock fights usually react with shock and yet with fascination.

Poultry that become pets are likely to be one of the varieties that are usually bred for food or show, although the pet bird rarely becomes a show bird and even more rarely ends up on the table.

The Rhode Island Red is a very popular breed because it is a very good layer and a very hardy bird. If it is crossed with a Light Sussex, birds for laying and the table can be produced. The Plymouth Rocks are large birds and also prolific layers; so too are the Barred and Buff Rocks.

More slightly built birds are the White, Black and Brown

The many domestic varieties of chicken are all strains of *Gallus gallus*, the Red Jungle Fowl. (*Above*) some of the variations; (*from left to right*) Barred Plymouth Rock, Minorca, Speckled Sussex, Rhode Island Red

Leghorns and the Ancona. The White Leghorn is a very good layer but the Black and the Ancona are preferred by people who live in towns because the birds do not show the dirt so easily.

When it is important to tell the sex of the birds at an early age North Holland Blues are frequently reared. The males are a lighter colour than the females and in about 80% of the chicks this can be seen as soon as they are hatched. Breeds where the cocks and hens are a different colour have been obtained by selective breeding between barred breeds and gold breeds, such as the Brown Leghorn or Buff Rock. The resulting cross is given a name that is a composite of its make up, such as Legbar of Buffbar.

Other varieties are kept and bred purely for their attractiveness – just like peacocks and pheasants. The most spectacular example is the long-tailed Yokohama, which comes from Japan. It has long elegant plumage and a tail that reaches 20 feet in length.

Bantams are diminutive breeds of the ordinary domestic hen, and like them can be had in many different breeds giving a whole range of attractive colours. They often start as pets because of their smallness and friendly nature, but here again it is the hens which are the best for family pet birds. Some bantam cockerels are extremely beautiful, yet they are equally as fierce, even if they are kept on their own, without an accompanying harem of hens. Their small size makes them very easy to handle, particularly by young people and, of course, their accommodation need only be quite small. They need the same general treatment as their larger brothers and sisters and react in much the same manner.

When chickens lived in a wild state their basic diet consisted of the seeds of wild plants, green plants, worms and insects. When they are kept in captivity the food supply is, therefore, limited and the natural diet must be supplemented.

(*From top to bottom*) Yokohama, Rose-crested Black Bantam, Black-tailed Japanese Bantam and (*right*) Black-breasted Bantam cock

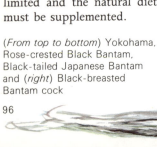

The various grains can be a mixture of wheat, maize, oats and barley and is especially useful if scattered in grass so the birds have to search to find it, thus getting exercise. Grain should only be fed along with a mixture of mash. Mash consists of several meals mixed together in various proportions. The type of mash depends on the age and type of chicken and is high in mineral elements.

Grit and lime are extremely important for these birds. If the diet is deficient in lime then soft-shelled eggs and bad plumage is the result. Eggshells, bone, oyster shell and limestone itself are all good sources of lime. The birds cannot chew their food but have a gizzard in which food can be ground up. They eat small stones which go into the gizzard and act as small millstones grinding up the food. If birds are able to range at will then they will be able to find enough

House for a single fowl. It is important
to have plenty of height for perching
and for wet weather there should be
a small outdoor walk adjacent to the
night box. Where a nest box is needed
this should be placed with a high
board near the perch to prevent the
bird fouling the box when perching.
The inside should be dug over often.

small stones, but, if not, then a trough of flint or grit must
be provided for them.

Finally, chickens often prove very good at waste disposal.
Kitchen scraps, especially potato peelings and other vegetable
waste can be boiled, mixed with mash and fed to the birds.

The housing of pet domestic poultry and bantams can be
very varied, and when only single birds of either kind are
kept, need not be very large. All that is needed is somewhere
that is dry and draughtproof, with a good firm perch, and
above all it must be easy to clean. Generally speaking, their
food and water vessels are placed outside as the birds
invariably have full liberty of a surrounding area. In some

cases old dog kennels have been converted and have been most suitable and accepted by the pet birds. Sometimes a bird will find its own sleeping spot in an old tree, underneath a raised building, or a niche in an old thick wall. If they do it is invariably best to leave them just where they like to be and not to attempt to put them in a specially prepared house.

Cleanliness is extremely important and the birds should be kept free from pests such as lice and fleas. To destroy pests, the birds should be dusted with a good insect powder several times during the summer. The houses can be creosoted against red mite.

Fresh water should always be available for drinking purposes. As for bathing, poultry differ from the normal kind of cage bird since they like to have a dust bath and a small patch of fine dry sand in one corner of the house will be much appreciated for this purpose.

A milk/bran mash is very suitable for poultry in the cold weather. Mashes of various kinds provide the birds with most of their protein.

Grain gives birds a lot of carbo-hydrate and supplies of already mixed corn can be bought. Birds should not be given too much or they will become fat.

Grit is used by birds to grind up the food they eat. Flint or granite grit is very suitable for it is hard and sharp.

Green foods are important providers of many of the birds' essential vitamins and minerals. Birds can be given cabbage, lettuce or other green vegetables to supplement a natural diet.

Ring-necked Pheasant
(*Phasianus colchicus*),
temperate Asia, 35 ins

Golden Pheasant (*Chrysolophus pictus*), central China highlands, 36 ins

Pheasants

Sometimes a wild Chinese or Ring-necked Pheasant is reared and tamed, but more often it is one of the so-called fancy pheasants that is taken for a pet. The majority of these birds are kept on very similar lines to the domestic poultry and bantams as indicated on pages 92 to 99. If a single cock bird of say a Golden, Silver or Lady Amherst's Pheasant is reared from a chick and kept at liberty in a large enclosed garden it can give the owner a lot of pleasure besides looking very beautiful. A hand-reared bird can become very tame and will quickly answer to its owner's call for food or tit-bits. Unless the birds are very tame most owners keep the wings clipped to prevent them from escaping and, of course, it must be realized that the garden must be quite a large one, with good areas of grass and lawn and a stout fence.

The Ring-necked Pheasant is one of the most widespread species of true pheasant and variation among individuals is considerable. The Golden Pheasant has been popular in

Silver Pheasant (*Gennaeus nycthemerus*), highlands of south eastern Asia, 39 ins

captivity for many years and it is made more suitable as a pet by the fact that it is a poor flier preferring to rely on its running speed and caution for its own safety. It is a hardy and simple bird to keep. Adult cocks will fight if kept together but if the wings are clipped and they are run in a large area with plenty of cover there will be only little fighting and they will make a wonderful display.

From old Chinese poetry the Silver Pheasant is known to have existed over 5,000 years ago. The large strikingly beautiful birds are popular as pets and the only disadvantage is that the cocks often fight when kept together. Several hens can be run with a cock, however, and at liberty in a garden they usually stay quite happily.

Lady Amherst's Pheasant is even more beautiful than its related species the Golden Pheasant. The general behaviour is very similar to the Golden Pheasant and what has been said of the one bird in captivity applies equally to the other except that the males may tend to be more pugnacious.

Swinhoe's Pheasant (*Lophura swinhoei*) originates from the island of Formosa but has now become rare in its native land. The first birds only reached Britain in the late 1950s but, since then, a large number of birds have been reared in captivity. So many in fact, that birds reared in captivity have been released in their native hills to supplement decreasing wild flocks. These birds do well in captivity and will breed easily, the chicks also being exceedingly easy to rear in captivity.

As an aviary bird, Reeve's Pheasant (*Syrmaticus reevesi*) is one of the easiest to keep and breed. Three hens can be run with a cock but the cock bird must be given a lot of room or else its extremely long tail feathers will soon be damaged. Because of this bird's vicious nature, however, this species should on no account be kept with other birds. They may also fight with one another if too closely confined.

At one time I reared a cock Lady Amherst's Pheasant, which had the liberty at first of our garden and later the surrounding fields. This bird was exceedingly tame and could be picked up at will, and it would always come to a special call; at the same time it was very friendly with our other animals. Its beautiful plumage was a great attraction for visitors, and it delighted in showing off in front of them. Other people who have kept pheasants have also found that they are most satisfactory pet birds and do not seem to

Lady Amherst's Pheasant (*Chrysolophus amherstiae*) is an attractive bird for a large garden. It comes from the south Tibet – upper Burma region and measures 50 ins.

trouble the garden area.

When pheasants are kept in an aviary this can be landscaped and planted with berry and flowering shrubs which will benefit the birds and show them off to advantage. The aviary should be in a sheltered and sunny position and, for most species, heavy shade should be avoided. Their food is simple; they need only a regular feeding of mixed corns as they find the green and grit together with insects in their wanderings round the garden. Chopped green food, such as lettuce, can also be offered together with apples or oranges. If insectivorous food is scarce they can be given live maggots or mealworms or some fresh, minced, raw beef. All in all, a pheasant is a most satisfying bird to keep in a reasonably-sized town or country enclosed garden.

Ducks

People of all ages seem to find ducks especially attractive and they often get great pleasure from feeding those that are kept in public places, such as parks and gardens. It is, in fact, unusual to discover a large open space of water that does not have its own special duck population. As a tame pet a duck is quite different in habits and temperament to domestic poultry and bantams. Most of them do not have the same flying power but they do have a strong liking for water.

The varieties of ducks, although not so numerous as poultry, nevertheless are quite extensive and vary considerably in their size and colour patterns. Specimens of many kinds will be found as individual pets but various crossbred birds seem to form the majority of the pet kinds, often crosses with the common Mallard. Like poultry chicks, newly

Mallard (*Anas platyrhynchos*), Europe, Asia and North America, 23 ins (*left*) and (*right*) Mandarin (*Aix galericulata*), north eastern Asia, 18 ins

This Mallard duckling shows no fear of humans. Adult ducks also tame very easily.

hatched ducklings are fluffy, pretty and most trusting towards human beings and naturally have a strong appeal to all young people.

Because of their natural behaviour, pet ducks must be kept as outside birds, once they get over their fluffy stage. Young ducks seem even more keen to attach themselves to their owners than other domesticated birds and come to rely on them to a far greater extent for their general care and feeding. The intensity of this attachment can at times be somewhat overwhelming, especially when they want to follow their owner everywhere, and at the same time rather quaintly pathetic.

Ducks are often the subject of many kinds of children's toys and these can range from small floating models for the bath to large wheeled pedal bicycles. They also frequently appear in cartoons, films on television and in books for young people.

All this contributes to making ducks so very attractive as pets to people of all ages, especially when they are small and covered with fluffy, yellow down. If it were not for the complications that can arise from keeping them in confined spaces, ducks could become very much more popular as pet birds.

As a general rule, a duck can only be satisfactorily kept as a pet if the owner has ample outside space available. However, its requirements are few and a pet duck needs only a small, low shelter for sleeping, a fairly large water vessel, and a bowl for food. The floor of the sleeping house should be well drained and covered with an absorbent material, such as sawdust, peat or a mixture of both, to facilitate easy cleaning. The main food of a pet can be household scraps

supplemented by some corn or poultry meal. As the pet should be kept with plenty of space at its disposal the bird will find naturally its own grit and green food. If this is not so supplies should then always be on hand.

Many pet ducks will form firm friendships with other domestic pets such as dogs, cats, goats, rabbits and even guinea-pigs. Great amusement can be had by watching another pet animal and a pet duck playing together quite unafraid and completely happy in their surroundings.

Although it is necessary for a duck always to have plenty of water to drink, a swimming place is not a must, but will

(*Left*) a portable duck night-house with removable side to facilitate cleaning out. There is a layer of peat on the floor which is absorbent and protects the bird's feet. Short legs on the house prevent damp. (*Below left*) plastic pond. (*Above*) Rouen drake a domestic breed from the Mallard

always be appreciated by most species. These days it is possible to get at garden centres or pet stores small pools made of plastic material which will serve as a pet's bathing place. These are generally moulded into an attractive shape. They can be situated in a hole dug in the ground and, although there is the problem of cleaning the water periodically if the pond is very small, it should need a minimum of

care and attention on the part of the owner.

If a small pond can be made, care should be taken to see that the surroundings are either made of stone or concrete. This surround should continue for a short distance below the water level. If this is not done then the area around the pool will soon become a mud patch from the ducks walking to and from the water. Sometimes one is lucky enough to have a small stream running through the garden. If this is the case, then a small area can be dammed or fenced off to make an ideal natural pond, although a concrete or stone 'slipway' should be provided as well.

A species of duck that is most popular as a pet is the Muscovy, which can be had in such colours as black, blue (grey), variegated and white. The commendable points about this variety are that they tame quickly, can easily be trained, do not fly much and do not seem to worry about having open water. It is rather strange that although in the ordinary way they do not fly much they have quite a powerful flight and can fly long distances should they feel so inclined.

Various colourings of the Muscovy Duck (*Cairina moschata*), South and Central America, 28-30 ins

Muscovies will crossbreed readily with most species of duck. Since the hybrids are sterile they are useful birds in mixed flocks where the numbers must be limited. One of the most frequent crosses is between a Muscovy and a Mallard (see page 104).

Mallards are very popular pets in their own right and have been reared in captivity for many hundreds of years. They are now distributed all over the world, with the exception of South America. Most of the birds that are kept on farms or as pets vary from the normal colour pattern of the wild species to white, black, blue (grey), fawn and multi-coloured specimens. Colour mutations are also frequent among the wild birds. Most Mallards settle down well in confinement and domestic birds can be seen to be much heavier than their wild relatives as well as having a much more tractable nature.

Call Ducks are miniature Mallards that are ornamental and attractive. The maximum weight is about $2\frac{1}{2}$ pounds and although most of the types kept seem to be white in colour, they can also be had in the same coloration as the wild Mallard. They are extremely strong and fast on the wing.

Another duck similar to the Mallard in coloration but much heavier is the Rouen Duck (see page 107). They are the easiest to manage of the heavier breeds of domestic duck.

The Mandarin drake (page 104) is one of the most ornamental birds in existence. In the wild state it is an Asiatic species of Wood Duck. It is an excellent duck for parks, gardens and aviaries and it can be kept without having its wings clipped with little danger that it will fly away. A pair can be kept in a small cage with a pond and will generally breed every spring.

The male Carolina Wood Duck, also known as the Gardinia Duck is another very beautiful bird that originated in North America. It is one of the most suitable species of duck that can be kept as a pet. It is a hardy bird and easily tamed, with little inclination to stray. It is also very tolerant towards other ducks and breeds easily. Carolinas and Mandarins should be provided with nesting boxes hung up on trees or poles near the water since, in the natural state, they nest in trees.

The Common Shelducks are a frequently observed species of salt-water areas and they are often seen on the shore eating molluscs and crustaceans as well as leaves and roots of aquatic plants. In captivity they thrive well providing they

(*Left*) Common Shelduck (*Tadorna tadorna*), Europe and Asia, 24 ins. (*Right*) White-faced Whistling, or Tree, Duck (*Dendrocygna viduata*), Africa and South America. 17-18 ins

have a large amount of land in which to find food naturally or else are provided with a rich mash. They need a fair amount of care but are hardy and breed well. The White-faced Tree, or Whistling, Duck is also common in collections and exceedingly tame although it breeds irregularly. Red-crested Pochards are also favoured ornamental birds and since they have similar requirements to mallards are often found together.

Whatever species of duck are kept as pets care should be taken to see that the pool is not overcrowded. If aggressive species are chosen the pool should be large enough so that the birds will not interfere with one another. Care should also be taken over the use of any weedkillers or soil or lawn dressings that are used in the garden. Pet birds have frequently been poisoned through eating greenstuff so treated.

Red-crested Pochard (*Netta rufina*), Europe and Central Asia, 22 ins

Carolina Wood, or Gardenia, Duck (*Aix sponsa*), North America, 20 ins

Geese

For many generations geese have been kept both as pets and watchdogs by people who live in country areas and those who are fortunate enough to have large gardens. The keeping of geese as pets goes far back into history and the Greylag Goose, probably one of the oldest domesticated birds, is figured on Egyptian frescos over 4,000 years old. Mutations occurred in wild birds that were reared in captivity and selective breeding has produced many of today's domestic forms.

There is much to recommend a goose besides its curious appearance and aptitude as a watchdog. They are so easy to keep because they are almost entirely vegetarians and will graze a small grass area like a lawn mower. There are many stories about geese scaring off intruders by their strong hissing noise, outstretched necks and widespread wings. Geese in this state can be quite fearsome but on the other hand they can be extremely tame and gentle with their owner and people they recognize. Their span of life compared with most birds is very great and some geese have been recorded of up to 25 or 30 years of age.

Geese threaten an intruder by extending the neck, lowering it to the ground and driving him away with much hissing and calling.

Three types of domesticated
goose; (*left to right*) Toulouse,
Emden and Chinese

Most people who have a pet goose provide it with a type
of shelter similar to that for a duck, but of course a little
larger to accommodate this larger-sized bird. However,
many tame specimens will absolutely ignore their shelter
and spend all their life both awake and asleep in the open
throughout the year.

The main food of geese, as already indicated, is grass but
they also like other fresh green foods such as lettuce, cabbage
or spinach. In addition they will take some grain, pellets or
poultry meal and foodstuffs that are usually fed to ducks.
It is important that they should also have access to flint and
limestone grit at all times.

In spite of the fact that most geese do not fly, it is surprising what a distance they will wander if given the opportunity, and it is therefore necessary to see that a pet goose is always safely enclosed. Although geese do not seem to require as much drinking water as ducks, they nevertheless must at all times have a constant supply of clean, fresh water available. Sometimes they will go on to water if there is any at hand but its absence does not appear to worry them in the least. They are certainly more dry-land birds than one would think, possibly because they are an artificially domesticated species.

The wild Brent and Greylag are at times to be found as pets and, although they make quite interesting ones too, the Canada Geese are much more amenable to human company. Canada Geese can fly very well indeed and this fact must be

Canada Goose (*Branta canadensis*), North America, 22-30 ins

borne in mind if one is taken as a tame pet. There are many sub-species and, although the larger forms breed more easily, they are aggressive during the breeding season and may be dangerous to other birds. The smaller forms are, on the other hand, inoffensive and are attractive in gardens. They interbreed freely with other geese.

The Brent Goose is a rather difficult species to raise well in captivity although they will live happily if plenty of grazing and some animal food is available. They are, however, very shy by nature and their coloration in comparison with most species of goose, is dull. Until recent years also, they had not been known to nest in captivity and thus, although a few are kept in large parks and gardens, they do not make very suitable pets.

Greylag Geese on the other hand have been domesticated for a long time and, although wild species are rare, all the tame breeds of geese (with the exception of the Chinese Geese) have been derived from them. The majority of these domestic geese are grey, white or partially coloured. The Emden Goose is a large white goose that originated in Germany and is now extensively raised. The males weigh about 20 pounds, the females a little less. Toulouse Geese are the largest of all the domestic geese and are now reared all over the world. The males can reach 30 pounds in weight.

The Chinese Goose is the domestic form of the Swan Goose (*Anser cygnoides*) and has proved more successful than the domestic forms of the Greylag in the warmer parts of the world. It is also called the African Goose.

(*Left*) Greylag Goose (*Anser anser*), northern and eastern Europe and central Asia, 32 ins. (*Right*) Brent Goose (*Branta bernicla*), north polar coastal areas, 24 ins

NATIVE BRITISH BIRDS

Jackdaws

Jackdaws will be found living wild in most areas of Britain. In some places they live in quite large colonies, even in the heart of towns and villages. For centuries Jackdaws have been tamed and are well known in legends, 'The Jackdaw of Rheims' being a famous one, for their mischievous habits of taking bright objects ranging from milk bottle tops to jewellery, in fact anything bright they can get in their beaks.

If taken into a home when young, a Jackdaw will become very tame and attached to its owner. This often happens to young birds which fall out of the nest and are rescued and hand reared by some kind person. Some birds are reasonably good at imitating other sounds and can even be trained to say the odd word or two, 'Jack' being the most common one learned. Most Jackdaws will live out of doors more or less at liberty coming to their owner for food when called. This

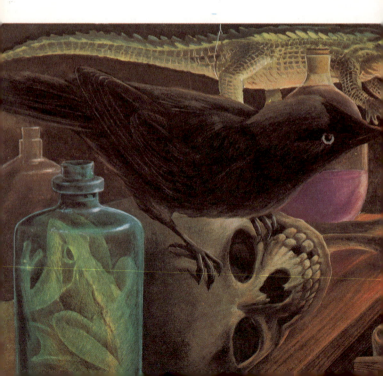

semi-domesticated state has been known to last for years and some birds will even go away and bring back a mate to share their own particular territory.

Jackdaws and other members of the family have in the past been associated with witchcraft and it was only in recent years that bird keepers took a different view of the Jackdaw. When in full plumage a Jackdaw is a handsome bird with its shining black coat, which it keeps immaculate for most of the year.

Jackdaws feed on all kinds of foods but must always have some percentage of meat and insects in their diet to keep them fit and well; this usually poses no problem in the ordinary household. As stated earlier, Jackdaws are notorious thieves and, therefore, a pet bird must not be allowed to have too much freedom in the house otherwise bright objects are liable to disappear and may not be found again.

The Jackdaw (*Corvus monedula*), Eurasia, 13 ins was often linked with many superstitions and supposed to be particularly associated with witches.

Ravens

In the olden days Ravens were often kept as pet birds at liberty outdoors in the grounds and surrounding areas of castles and other large establishments. They were also kept as single pets by learned men, alchemists and their like and were considered by the people of those times to be birds of strange powers. At this period Ravens were breeding quite freely in many areas of Britain but today owing to industrial and agricultural developments their breeding grounds are few and very limited, and wild specimens are rarely seen except by bird-watchers. Ravens are often mentioned in books including, of course, the Bible, which contains references to these birds on several occasions, thus indicating what an important place ravens had in the lives of human beings.

Today Ravens are only seen by the general public in zoological gardens and parks, and without a doubt the most famous Ravens in Britain are those birds that live in the Tower of London. This little flock is part of the establishment and is jealously cared for by the keepers of the Tower. Thousands of visitors from all over the world are always

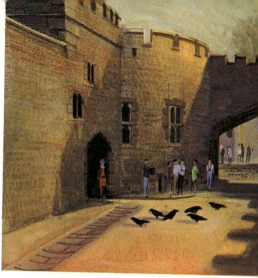

The Raven (*Corvus corax*), northern hemisphere, 25 ins.
(*Above*) Ravens at the Tower of London outside the Bloody
Tower. Legend says that, if they leave, the White Tower will fall
and a great calamity will affect the country.

amazed to see these birds freely wandering in the courtyards
quite unconcernedly.

The Carrion Crow (*Corvus conore conore*) is similar to the
Raven but can be distinguished by its smaller size and
thinner beak. It is sometimes kept as a pet and individuals
may become quite tame. Generally they are not a very
attractive bird with a rasping call.

The crow family in general, with the exception of the Jay
(*Garrulus glandarius*), are not particularly specialized as to
the type of food that they eat. They will often eat carcasses
of dead animals and the Raven has been known to attack
sick animals such as rabbits or lambs. They will all steal the
eggs of other birds. Most of these birds have been attacked
by man for the damage and harm that they are supposed to
do, although this damage has probably been exaggerated.
The truth probably lies in the fact that these appear such
unattractive birds. All, except the Raven, have managed to
hold their own in this struggle, however, and this is a good
example of their adjustability.

Owls

A finger tame young Little Owl (*Athene noctua*), Europe, Northern Africa and central Asia 8½ ins

These are birds which over the years have also been associated with various kinds of magic, and owls have actually been kept as pets for many more centuries than most of the birds that are known so well today. At one time owls were always connected with witches, church towers, caves and ruined buildings, but nowadays it is usually in childrens stories that they are featured. This is probably because of their nocturnal habits, silent flight and quaint flat faces with large unwinking eyes.

The Barn Owl (*Tyto alba*),
North and South
America, Europe, Africa,
Southern Asia and
Australia, 15-17 ins

It can well be imagined that there are drawbacks to having a pet owl. A great many people do not have the accommodation or the means to provide their food. Young owls, deserted by their parents, are sometimes reared by country people, who keep them in outhouses as semi-tame pets for many years. Once reared, such birds will generally obtain the majority of their own food by hunting at night. When they are being hand reared, raw meat is generally used as a basic diet. This food does not give the birds all they require, since they need some kind of roughage such as feathers, hair or small bones to form the pellets which they eject after they have absorbed the necessary nourishment from their food. Some feathers or hair should therefore be mixed with the raw meat, supplementing this with an occasional dead mouse.

At one time it was the Barn Owl that was the species mainly kept as a pet, but nowadays it would seem that the smaller Little Owls are more favoured. Possibly the size of these latter make them more easy to handle and seem more suitable to have as pets.

A tame Magpie (*Pica pica*),
Eurasia and western North
America, 18 ins

Magpies

Some few years ago Magpies were much more frequently kept as pets than they are at the present time. Their mischievous nature both in the wild and in captivity has over the years made them the subject of numerous stories both for adults and children.

At the present the few are kept as pets make most attractive ones with their clear cut, glossy black and white colouring and long tapering tails. Most of these birds become pets through being found as deserted young, when their nest has been destroyed by high winds or hedge clearance. They are the only large species of bird in Britain that make a nest with a covered top.

Magpies take kindly to a life in captivity and their owners seem to have no trouble in getting them to take food when first taken in hand. Their appetite is large and they will thrive on a very mixed diet ranging from canary soft food to shredded meat, fish, and all kinds of other household scraps, together with live insects both large and small. Even when fully adult their appetites are still very large and their feeding materials should be even more varied.

A tame Magpie can be housed in a large cage, an aviary, or at semi-liberty in a barn or out-building. One particular feature of their care is that pet Magpies do not seem to take much interest in bathing like most other species of bird.

If the prospective pet owner has the opportunity of taking and rearing a young Magpie from the nestling stage, a very amusing pet can be easily trained. Most Magpies are very amenable to animals and often form strong friendships with other household pets. They also seem to be especially attached to children, although this is possibly because children often feed the birds with all sorts of odd things and being rather greedy by nature magpies are attracted by this treatment. Because of the nature of their foodstuff and also the fact that they are best kept at liberty, however, it must be realized that Magpies are best kept as outside pets and their presence in the house is not really desirable.

Magpies build large domed nests, frequently near farms. They are often adorned with shiny objects.

Hawks

As stated at the beginning of this book hawks of various kinds are probably man's oldest captive birds, and at one time held a most distinguished place in all the households where they were maintained. Although hawks have been kept by men for so long, they really cannot be considered in the same category as most other tame pet birds. Even though they become very gentle and friendly with their owners their fierce attitude towards other people and their diet of flesh make them impracticable as true pets. In fact they must be classed as sporting birds, like hunting dogs and cheetahs are sporting animals. Quite often dogs, or Cheetahs, and hawks are used in co-operation with each other in the same hunts, particularly in the eastern countries where such sporting activities are still practised.

The generalized name hawk is specifically used to mean the true hawks, which include the Goshawk (*Accipiter gentilis*) the kites and harriers, and also the falcons such as the Peregrine Falcon (*Falco peregrinus*). The choice of any particular species for

The training of hawks and falcons is extremely complex and requires much patience and experience. Each species requires a specialized system of training. Some falconers breed their own hawks in captivity so they will not have to rely on wild birds but, generally, these birds are not easily domesticated. Legislation in most countries is favourable towards falconry.

training is usually a matter of preference on the part of the owner. Their large relatives, the eagles, are also on rare occasions reported as being taken in as pet birds. Because of their great size and strength, however, they can only be kept by people with extensive knowledge of the management of such birds.

Most of the more popular kinds of birds that are universally kept as domestic pets have now been dealt with fairly fully, as well as some of those less frequently encountered under domestic conditions. However, there are a few more species on which a few words must be said, as they are sometimes tamed to a considerable degree in various parts of the world.

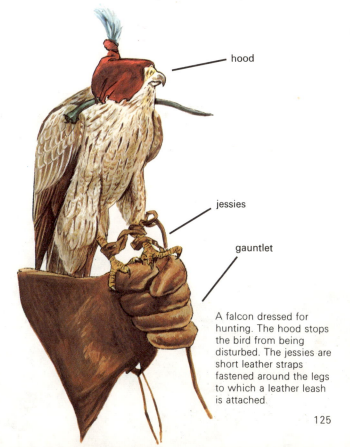

hood

jessies

gauntlet

A falcon dressed for hunting. The hood stops the bird from being disturbed. The jessies are short leather straps fastened around the legs to which a leather leash is attached.

125

UNUSUAL PET BIRDS

Ostriches

The largest by far of all the many birds of the world is the flightless Ostrich; the males of which can stand up to 8 feet in overall height and weigh some 300 pounds. In spite of their size they are quite gentle when tamed and can be put to domestic uses. Some specimens are trained to pull light, two-wheel carts, like trotting horses and they can become very fast and skilful at this kind of work, although when tired they will usually sit down and refuse to move whatever persuasion is used. Ostrich racing is a popular sport in some parts of America and the birds are ridden and pitted against each other like racehorses. At some zoological gardens they are fitted with light saddles and children ride upon their backs.

Ostriches live well in captivity and have about the same

(*Left*) Ostriches (*Struthio camelus*), come from the African plains, are about 72 ins long and stand about 8 feet. The female is slightly lighter in colour. (*Above*) saddle used in Ostrich riding.

life-span as humans. Captive populations are most frequently kept to supply the demand for their plumage. The commercial plumes are only those that grow on the wings or tail. The birds grow a new set each year. Farms were first established in Africa and birds were later exported to North and Central America.

Because of their size and curious shape it is difficult to think of Ostriches as being birds, let alone pet birds, but nevertheless people who have kept Ostriches maintain that they are quite easy to handle and soon become very friendly with their owners.

Their feeding is quite simple as they are vegetarians, but nevertheless they are not adverse to eating many other kinds of foods and also other things. The objects that have been removed from the crops and gizzards of Ostriches at some time or another are truly remarkable, ranging from uncut diamonds to gold watches, coins, childrens' small toys and iron nails. This peculiar eating habit has made the Ostrich the subject of a whole host of really amusing bird stories.

127

Peafowl

 For many centuries Peafowl of various kinds have been
kept in captivity or at semi-liberty as tame ornamental pet
birds in a number of countries of the Old World. They are
mentioned in the Bible and various other books, both ancient
and modern, and especially when pride is alluded to. The
Persians seem to be particularly fond of the peacock motif
in their paintings, carpets and metal-ware, and it is also
frequently seen in the art of many other countries. Because
they are so easily domesticated most zoos have them wandering freely and since ancient times the Hindu religion has
protected the peafowl.

 The adult males have a vividly coloured and beautifully
patterned plumage with the long tail being an outstanding

feature. In full breeding plumage these tails are some 4 feet in length, and when the birds get excited or indulge in courtship display they are erected and spread, forming a circle of feathers behind their heads. This fanning of the long tail feathers gives a most wonderful, 'eyed', patterned effect and shows to full advantage the rich colours in symmetrical array. It is from this display that the simile 'as proud as a peacock' comes. The peahens are considerably smaller than their colourful mates and their colouring appears to be rather drab in comparison.

Peafowl are quite easy to keep in Britain and require the minimum of attention all through the year. Except in very large gardens or estates, most people only keep a single peacock for ornamental purposes. A bird kept on its own in

The Common, or Indian Peafowl (*Paro cristatus*), India and Ceylon, 80-92 ins including tail

a garden will soon become friendly with its owner, will come when called and will display its beautiful colours to the enjoyment of all present.

A single pet bird will usually manage to get most of its own food but will need a small daily allowance of corn, which should be increased during the winter months. Their other food consists of grasses, green and seeding weeds and all kinds of insects. A peacock will find for itself a sheltered roosting-place and always seems to prefer this to a man-made shelter. They possess rather a weird call and when uttered at night or early morning it has been confused with ghostly cries! Owners of peafowl usually find them the most untroublesome of ornamental birds that can be kept at liberty in an enclosed garden.

Penguins

Of the flightless birds, penguins are without a doubt the most popular with both old and young in all countries. Everyone seems fascinated by their curiously shaped, erect bodies, slow almost human walk, immense speed and mobility in water, and above all their fearless attitude towards human beings.

There are many different species of penguins. They all have the same characteristics, varying only in size and colouring. All varieties of penguins come from the southern hemisphere and are not known in the northern, although the climatic conditions are very similar in both regions. In the wild they live in tremendous colonies and they have inhabited their breeding areas for countless years.

Owing to their gregarious habits, special housing conditions and food, penguins are not suitable as single pets and are consequently usually kept in small colonies in zoological gardens or on large estates where collections of different birds are housed.

Emperor and King Penguins are the largest and most colourful species. They

(*Above*) Humboldt or Peruvian Penguin (*Spheniscus humboldti*), western South American coasts from the Falklands to Peru, about 20 ins

both have vivid ear patches. The King's are a golden colour, the Emperor (*Aptenodytes forsteri*) has orange-yellow patches. Emperors are only slightly taller than King Penguins but about twice the weight.

A penguin often seen in zoos is the Jackass Penguin (*Spheniscus demersus*), which is 26 inches long and has a black band across its chest. Very similar to this is the Humboldt Penguin; another popular zoo animal and slightly smaller in size.

(*Right*) Macaroni Penguin (*Eudyptes chrysolophus*), New Zealand, about 2 ft. (*Below*) Blackfooted, or Jackass, Penguin (*Spheniscus demersus*) South African islands, 28 ins

(*Opposite*) King Penguin (*Aptenodytes patagonicus*),subantarctic islands, 38 ins. (*Extreme right*) Little Blue, or Fairy Penguin (*Eudyptula minor*), Australia and New Zealand, 12 ins

In their natural environment penguins will feed on animals caught near to the sea surface. These include crustacea, small shoaling fish and larval fish forms. They have also been known to feed on squid. Particular species can be associated with particular foods but no particular link with the shape of the bill can be deduced. In captivity penguins will soon learn to eat frozen fish slices although they may have to be forcibly fed in the early stages.

Swans

As ornamental water birds, swans are perhaps the most picturesque of all the tame species and throughout the centuries they have been the source of inspiration to the various arts. Although many people will add a pair of swans to a stream or lake in their grounds, it is not unusual nowadays for a pair to suddenly appear on their own. Because of the protection these birds now receive their numbers have increased enormously over the past few years.

Unlike most birds, swans mate for life and, when their young become fully grown, the old birds drive them away from their territory. This means that the young birds must find a territory for themselves and consequently they will settle on any water that is untenanted by other swans. There is hardly a public garden or park in Britain that possesses a stretch of water that does not have its own swans. These may range from a solitary bird on a small area of water to several breeding pairs where the water space is

Mute Swan (*Cygnus olor*), Eurasia, 60 ins. The cygnets often ride on their parents' backs.

large enough for each individual pair to have its own feeding territory.

Swans are usually omnivorous and generally speaking it is the amount of food available that controls the number of pairs of birds of any kind that inhabit a particular area. This is the reason why in some parts of the country there are say half a dozen pairs of one kind of bird and yet in another there is only one pair populating the same area of ground.

For most part of the year swans are very tame and friendly and will take food gently from the hands of children or adults when offered. For a short time each spring the most tame of swans may become a little aggressive while their mates are sitting on eggs. When the babies have hatched the tameness soon returns.

Some swans live as single pets in the grounds of large houses where conditions are suitable. Such birds are perfectly happy and contented on their own.

Black Swan (*Chenopis atrata*), Australia, 56-60 ins and (*right*) Blacknecked Swan (*Cygnus melanocoryphus*) South America, 42 ins

Toucans

Although these rather strangely-shaped birds, which are called toucans, have been kept by experienced aviculturists for a very long time, it is only in recent years that they have become well known to the general public. Many toucans start their lives in captivity with a family just as ordinary interesting cage birds along with other exotic species. However, in many cases it is not long before their quaintness and friendliness make them one of the owner's special pets. In spite of their confiding ways with human beings they can be very pugnacious towards each other when kept in captivity and must always be housed separately.

Most of the species of toucans – they all originally came from South America – are quite large birds, some of them over 20 inches in length. A popular species is the Toco Toucan which is about 22 inches in length including a beak some 9 inches long. The Green-billed Toucan is slightly smaller and although it is rarely found in collections it does make a very suitable pet. The smaller toucanets such as the Spot-billed Toucanet are often easier to keep in captivity

(*Right*) Green-billed Toucan (*Ramphastos dicolorus*), South America, 20 ins and (*below*) Spot-billed Toucanet (*Selenidera maculirostris*), Brazil, 11 ins

because of their size, but are more susceptible to cold weather. All Toucans have large beaks which look as if they can be dangerous if used in anger or defence; however, although these beaks appear massive they are mainly hollow, fibrous structures and cannot give a really effective bite.

Toucans are mainly fruit-eating species and their diet can include all kinds of fruits of the drier kinds such as figs, dates, hard apples and sultanas, and soft fruits should be given more sparingly together with some dried insectivorous food or raw meat. Because of their foodstuffs they are not particularly good birds to be kept ordinarily as indoor pets but can be housed satisfactorily on a terrace, verandah or some such shelter. They should be given a large flight area or regularly allowed the freedom of a room. Although reasonably hardy, they cannot stand cold or damp and must always have a suitable dry shelter as well as water for bathing in if they wish. In summer they often take sand baths and a dish of dry sand should be provided if they are kept in a cage inside. Although popular pets and common in zoos, Toucans have never been known to breed in captivity.

Toco, or Giant, Toucan (*Ramphastos toco*), South America, 22 ins

CAGES AND BUILDINGS

Since pet birds vary so greatly in their habits and size, the types of housing must vary directly with the type of pet. Some birds are kept in pens or aviaries for breeding purposes but usually their owners keep them only for decorative and amusement purposes and their housing is often up to individual taste. In the comments on the birds in the previous pages, specific requirements have been noted and the following is a discussion of some further points of construction and materials that have a general bearing on the subject.

All cages and houses should be of simple design so that they are easy to clean by the owner and simple to redecorate when necessary. Any painted areas should be covered with a non-poisonous enamel paint or plastic emulsion. The colour of the paint is up to the owner's taste. If a distemper is used a disinfectant can be added and it will help reduce the possibility of insect pests. If the birds are to be maintained in a fit healthy state it is most important that their abode does not contain unnecessary lurking places for unpleasant germs or lice.

When the all-wire type of cage is being used it should be constructed of the best quality material and its design should

Selection of all-wire and box-type cages

be firm and solid. If the wirework is painted instead of being chromium plated it must be of a good high gloss finish. Sometimes wire cages are available with parts covered in plastic. These cages are more difficult to keep clean as the plastic coating frequently gets chipped either by the birds themselves or in usage. A good, well-made, first quality all-wire cage is probably the best buy in most instances and is easy to keep clean and will last in good condition for many years.

As we have already seen some species of birds are best housed in the wood and wire box-type cage. Wire fronts are made in many sizes and in fact are the complete wire-work, including doors, of a cage. With a box of appropriate size and shape these fronts permit very cheap cages to be constructed. Many pet shops also have special 'cage sets', which are all the essential requirements ready for construction. With such cages the woodwork should be of good quality, well-seasoned wood that is as free as possible from knots and cracks. The wood should be given several coats of a non lead-containing paint or an emulsion paint so as to fill in and seal off any small cracks or crevices that could shelter mites. In addition, if the cage woodwork is well painted, it is so easy to wash thereby keeping it in a perfectly clean condition.

When cages of any kind are being washed, warm water and a good germicide should be used for the purpose. After washing the cages should be thoroughly rinsed with plain warm water and allowed to get really dry, perhaps using a fan heater or hair dryer, before the birds are put back.

Correct perching in cages is most important and every endeavour should be made to see that they are of different thicknesses. It is easy to realize that, if all the perches in a cage are of the same diameter, the feet of the birds cannot get properly exercised and a great deal of stiffness in the feet of small caged birds is due to improper perching.

These perches can be made of machined wood, which can be bought at pet shops in various diameters both in oval and round shapes. In addition, perches made from natural wood are very useful and these should be obtained from fruit trees, hazel bushes, wild plum, whitethorn, elm, hornbeam and larch. Care should be taken to avoid woods that are likely to splinter and perches should be watched to see that this does not occur. Such woods as oak, ash or lilac should only be used in their thoroughly dry state after the bark, which is poisonous, has been stripped off them. With some of the parrot-like birds these natural perches are very beneficial and their use is thoroughly recommended. This does mean that they must be frequently renewed but, nevertheless, the birds do get benefit from eating the wood and also exercise their beaks.

Perches must be securely fixed so the birds can move confidently on them and so positioned as to give the birds as much flight space as possible as well as varied distances between perches. Care should also be taken to see that they are not positioned directly above one another, or over food or drinking vessels. If this were so then they are likely to foul either their dishes or the birds beneath them. Too many perches must also be avoided as accidents can occur when the birds cannot get enough flying room.

Cages should be cleaned regularly and the best method (*right*) is to wash them with warm water with added disinfectant. All moveable parts and attachments should also be washed separately, everything being thoroughly dried before the bird is returned.

Various shapes of
machine and natural
perches

The food and water vessels for cages can generally be bought at the right sizes from pet shops and there is usually a vast range of shapes and sizes. With the smaller birds it is essential to have all vessels inside the cage to prevent losses by escaping, even if it does mean that they need changing more frequently. These should always be kept perfectly clean to prevent infection. It is very necessary during the summer months to wash these vessels almost daily, particularly those for containing water.

The materials used for covering the floors of all-wire or box-type cages that contain the seed-eating birds can be sand, coarse pine sawdust, a mixture of both, or special sanded sheets. Pet birds always seem to get much more benefit if they have ordinary bird sand on their cage floors as this contains various grits and minerals that they would not get otherwise. If the sand is obtained from natural pits, river beds, or the seashore, care should be taken to see that it is perfectly clean and has not been fouled in any way. If sanded sheets are used then it is best for the birds that some grit is sprinkled over the sheets. If this is done then the birds can peck about for it should they wish to do so.

Softbilled birds require a different technique for the cleaning and covering of their cage floors. If it is possible the owner should arrange for the cage to have two separate loose bottom trays so that one can be in use while the other is being changed. The covering should be of a good absorbent material which must be changed very frequently. With many of these species a good layer of newspaper on the tray floor covered with a piece of blotting paper is very economical and very absorbent. A single piece of blotting paper is frequently not sufficient to soak up the surplus moisture from the droppings of the bird. With some of the larger types of birds that have a diet of only some soft foods, peat or a

(*Left*) various types of food dispensers that can be obtained from pet shops. (*Right*) drinking vessels; the bottom right can be used for either seed or water.

mixture of peat and sand can be used to advantage.

The materials used for making larger cages, pens and aviaries, that are to house outside pet birds can be many and varied but in all cases like the cages the design should be simple and they should be easy to clean. Brick, wood, hardboard or plaster board can all be used and sometimes a mixture of these materials will be found useful. The roof can be covered by felt or one of the new fibre-glass materials according to the species of bird to be housed. Here again the whole structure should be decorated both inside and out with either a lead-free paint or emulsion paint. In certain cases creosote or some other wood-preserving fluid can be used externally.

Perches can again be made of manufactured wood or natural branches according to the variety of bird to be housed in the structure, and once again attention should be paid to seeing that the perches vary in their thicknesses. For birds that do not have strong gnawing beaks almost any

1. Converted small coach-house to hold doves and pigeons in the loft. An outdoor flight is added to the warmer south side. Since the interior is large enough to walk in it could hold different types of the larger varieties of birds. 2. A small outdoor flight on the terrace of a modern bungalow to hold Budgerigars. 3. A derelict Victorian conservatory suitable for conversion into a birdhouse. 4. A converted summerhouse to hold finches. 5. Built-up flight around a dead tree suitable for British softbills

kind of natural wood branches can be used for perches.

The seed and water vessels should be of a size comparable to the size of the bird kept and they too should be always washed frequently so that they do not get dirty and form traps for germs. With larger types of birds, although the water vessels should be of reasonable size, they should be of the shallow type in preference to the tall jam jar style. If there is any likelihood of the birds knocking over the water or the seed vessels they should be firmly fixed to prevent this happening.

Where ground-living birds are kept in a shelter it is of utmost importance to see that the floor of their shelter is well-drained. If it is made of concrete then it should have a good thick covering of sawdust, sand and sawdust, or peat. There is nothing that upsets a bird more quickly than having to sleep and live on the ground that is wet and sticky. In some cases, owners construct a low, slatted, wooden platform for their birds to sleep on and this is generally appreciated. Very frequently, when ground-living birds are allowed to roam around grounds or garden quite freely, they find their own particular place to roost at night. Nevertheless the owner should see that somewhere dry is provided for the bird should it wish to return there.

Aviaries should always be in a sunny sheltered position and, if the space is available, large, open-topped pens are probably the best enclosure. The wire sides of such pens should be dug into the ground for about a foot and the sides overhang outwards at the top to prevent predators climbing in. Small movable pens are often constructed so that the birds can frequently be transferred to fresh pasture. These are particularly important for grazing birds but well-drained land is essential for the success of this method.

It can be seen from the above descriptions that owners can use all types of structures for housing their birds, employing as much imagination as they wish, providing that certain essential rules are carried out for the birds' comfort and for their hygiene.

Wire runs and shelters. (*Above*) an all-year-round aviary for small birds converted from a standard greenhouse. Half the greenhouse is left glassed for a winter flight, the other half is enclosed for nesting boxes and night cages. The added summer flight takes the same shape as the greenhouse. (*Left*) nighthouse and run for large ground birds. The wire enclosure at the top of the run eliminates wing-clipping. (*Below*) an enclosure built near running water for ducks. The wire gate prevents vermin entering the night box.

AILMENTS

If the tame pet bird is a fit and healthy specimen to begin with and well housed and correctly fed, it will rarely suffer from any illness. However, occasionally the odd bird may fall sick for reasons beyond the owner's control and, this being so, the following paragraphs outline some of the symptoms and suggested treatment.

When any pet bird is seen to be unwell, and this is generally indicated by the bird looking fluffed up, drowsy, eyes dull, and with loose droppings, it should be isolated from all other birds and kept warm. This is the first step that should be taken with all suspected cases of sickness with any kind of bird.

Before starting treatment, the cage or house, perches, seed and water vessels and any toys, should be thoroughly disinfected by washing with a solution of an antiseptic and warm water, to stop re-infection and further spread. It is also advisable for the owner to wash his or her hands every time the sick bird, or its cage, is touched. This is a further preventative measure against reinfection.

The following are some specific illnesses applicable to certain groups of birds with suggestions for their treatment.

Birds that are suffering from a cold, or are generally sick, usually sit miserably on the bottom of their cage.

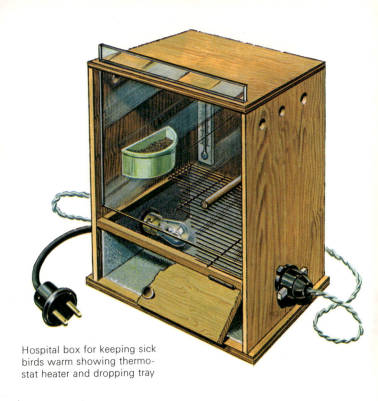

Hospital box for keeping sick
birds warm showing thermo-
stat heater and dropping tray

Colds, chills or catarrh

All kinds of birds whether outdoor or indoor pets may at
some period of their lives develop a cold. This can be due to
a draught, excessive change of temperature, loss of feathers
through moulting, a sudden cold wind, or by being contracted
from another sick bird. The usual symptoms of a cold are
difficulty in breathing through the nostrils, sneezing, and a
general air of dejection. The sick bird should be kept warm
and one of the patent cold cures, as supplied by pet shops,
suitable for the particular bird should be given as directed.

If the instructions are followed carefully the patient will
soon recover and be fit and well again. If the bird has been
taken indoors from outside then it will be necessary to
harden off the bird gradually before putting it back into
its old quarters.

Yellow-naped Amazon Parrot
in heavy moult

Moulting

All species of birds periodically moult all their feathers but
this is not an illness but a natural function; however, during
the process of losing their old feathers and gaining new ones
any bird is liable to contract a chill if not given special
attention. A moulting bird should not be subjected to
draughts or sudden changes of atmospheric conditions. The
growing of new feathers imposes an extra physical strain on
a bird and, therefore, it will need extra nourishment during
that period. In addition to vitamin-containing foods, a bird
should be given plenty of fresh green foods (or fruit) and
mineral-containing elements. During the moulting period the
bird should not be handled more than necessary and should
be allowed long periods of restful quietness. Generally
speaking, a complete moult takes five to seven weeks
according to the species but it may take a little longer as a
bird gets older. Many house pets have small partial moults
at various times of the year usually due to sudden climatic
changes but these are not serious and do not harm the bird
in any way. It is thus obvious, that it is best to maintain a
household pet in an even temperature.

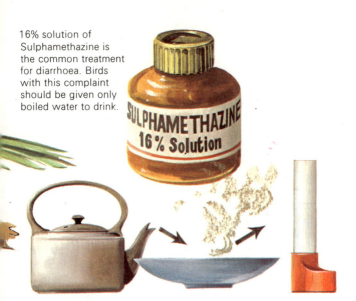

16% solution of Sulphamethazine is the common treatment for diarrhoea. Birds with this complaint should be given only boiled water to drink.

Diarrhoea

This rather distressing condition can accompany many other ailments and at the same time can be developed on its own. The symptoms of diarrhoea are very obvious and it necessitates the sick bird's cage being cleaned very frequently. Should any of the bird's vent or other feathers become soiled they should be gently washed clean with a disinfectant and warm water. If this is not done the bird may reinfect itself when endeavouring to clean its feathers. Once again, warmth is essential and, with birds that eat green food, this should be discontinued while the stomach is upset. There are numerous patent medicines on the market all of which are good but they do not seem to act in every case because of the differences in the cause of the trouble. If a medicine has not proved successful, then Sulphamethazine, 16% solution, should be given as prescribed by a veterinary surgeon. The sick bird should be fed on a plain simple diet and all tit-bits should be withheld until the condition has completely cleared. In cases of diarrhoea it is usually best to give the birds water that has first of all been boiled and then has been allowed to cool.

Constipation

It is not very often that pet birds suffer from constipation but occasionally Canaries, British birds and some of the parrot-like species may be fed too much rich dry foods and develop this condition. In softbilled species over-rich food or a badly balanced diet can also cause constipation. Usually it can be cleared within a very short space of time by giving a bird extra green food or fruit as the case may be. Sometimes, however, this treatment will not have the desired results and the bird will still be seen to be in difficulty. The addition of a drop of cod-liver oil to the seed or a few crystals of Epsom salts in the drinking water will invariably cure the bird. Another quick cure is the giving to two drops of castor-oil straight into the beak with the aid of a fountain pen filler. No special heat treatment is necessary.

Constipation should never be confused with eggbinding, which is a serious condition in hen birds, usually occurring with the first egg. There are many suggestions for treatment including holding the bird over steam but usually it is best to call in the help of a veterinary surgeon.

Constipated birds should be given a few grains of some health salts in their drinking water. (*Opposite*) the vent of birds suffering from enteritis should be cleaned with a soft brush.

Enteritis

This serious inflamatory condition of the intestines must not be confused with the more milder form of diarrhoea. There are two forms, contagious and non-contagious the former being caused by a germ, the latter by food poisoning. Enteritis can be caused by any bird eating mouldy, contaminated or stale food, particularly during hot weather. Another source of infection can be through the water where green food or soft food is allowed to ferment. The droppings in the case of enteritis are usually very fluid, copious, green-tinted and may be foul-smelling. It is important that whatever kind of bird is suffering from enteritis it should be taken into a warm even temperature and its feathers should they be fouled washed with a disinfectant and warm water. It may also be necessary with some species to wash the feet and legs. In my opinion unless the owner is well versed in bird sickness it is always best to call in a veterinary surgeon for advice if enteritis is suspected. The usual conditions of hygiene as previously mentioned should be strictly observed.

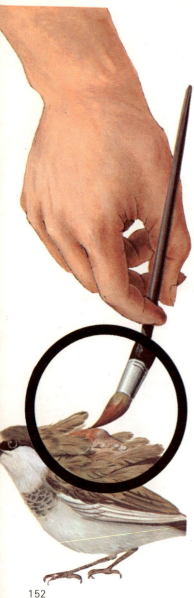

Tumours

Many different kinds of birds may at odd times develop small tumours on back, wings, or chest, and occasionally on the soft parts of the body. It is usually possible for the owner to treat a small tumour on a bird's back, wings or chest, by painting it once every eight days with tincture of iodine, and adding four drops of the same tincture every fourth day to the drinking water. This treatment should be continued until the growth has been reduced or completely cleared. Sometimes tumours on the upper parts of the body can be removed by a veterinary surgeon. It may happen that, occasionally, birds will develop septic spots. These can usually be removed and the area treated with a little iodine. Care should be taken to see that anything that is used for treatment of such an ailment is sterilized first. Should the owner have any doubt about any particular growth, then it is important that he seeks expert advice from a veterinary surgeon immediately.

A tumour can often be treated satisfactorily by painting it once a week with tincture of iodine.

Scaly Face

Scaly Face is a condition that is found in Budgerigars and is of a similar origin to Scaly Leg in domestic poultry. Scaly Face is caused by a minute boring insect and affects the beak, cere, and the skin that surrounds the eyes. It usually first appears as small whitish crumb-like growths at the side of the beak; these develop and spread over the cere, beak, and on to the eye skin. Occasionally the feet and legs may be affected and here it is seen by whitish lumps and the raising of the leg scales. It is possible for a bird to have Scaly Face but its presence not being revealed for many months after the bird has been bought. Fortunately this condition can be quickly and completely cured by applying one of the patent Scaly Face creams or ointments as directed. Scaly Leg can usually be cleared up by applying tepid water with a brush and then dabbing with turpentine. The scales drop off when the mites have been killed. To prevent reinfection, anything the bird has been in contact with must be washed with disinfectant and hot water, rinsed in cold running water and dried well.

Scaly Face and Scaly Leg are caused by a minute insect and result in whitish, scale-like growths. Many creams and ointments are available for clearing up the trouble.

Clipping beaks and claws

Many of the smaller types of birds that are kept as indoor pets are liable to suffer from overgrown beaks and claws through lack of something that would be provided in the natural environment. When it is observed that the beak of a pet has grown too long for it to eat comfortably it should be cut back with the aid of a small pair of sharp scissors. Mortar, cuttlefish bones and various minerals nibbles should, usually, prevent this condition happening, or recurring. It is important that only the surplus horny growth should be cut

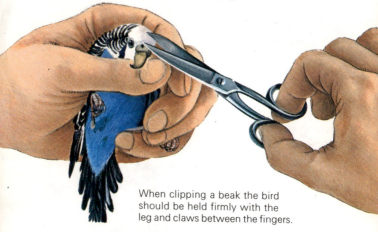

When clipping a beak the bird should be held firmly with the leg and claws between the fingers.

away and not the beak itself otherwise it may cause bleeding. Should claws become over-long and then not be clipped to a reasonable length, the pet may get its foot caught up and hurt itself seriously. If the claws are held to the light a small vein will be seen running through the centre and the cut should be made just beyond the end of the vein so that bleeding does not occur. Here again sharp scissors are essential. The cause of overgrown claws is very frequently too small perching in a cage which provides little opportunity for them to be worn down normally. If this happens steps should be taken to vary the size of the perches, perhaps providing natural wood perches if it is at all possible.

Wounds

Occasionally the pet bird will suffer some kind of injury through coming into contact with something sharp in the house or by fighting with other birds. In most cases the best treatment for ordinary cuts is to gently mop up the area with an antiseptic and warm water and then apply a bland ointment or dust with boracic powder. Should a wing or a leg get broken or there be large cuts that need stitching then it is best to call in the expert advice of a veterinary surgeon immediately.

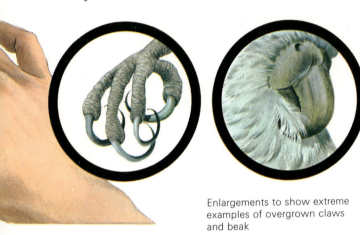

Enlargements to show extreme examples of overgrown claws and beak

The object of this book has been to explain what delightful pets can be made of the many species of birds from all over the world. Birds have been man's companions for countless centuries and in these hectic times their presence in a household has a comforting and soothing effect. A pet bird has often transformed the whole outlook of otherwise lonely people by its song, cheerful ways or its ability to imitate the human voice. Whatever species of bird that is kept as a pet, its real value depends to a great extent on the kind treatment and understanding it receives from its owner. In fact, as the friendship develops, man and bird become more and more dependent on each other for companionship.

BOOKS TO READ

The following books are useful introductions and guides to the recognition and care of various birds. They are usually available from bookshops and public libraries.

A – Z of Budgerigars by C. H. Rogers. Max Parish, London, 1961.

A Guide to Pheasants of the World by Philip Wayre. Country Life, London, 1969.

Australian Birds by R. Hill. Nelson, Melbourne, 1967.

Australian Finches in Bush and Aviary by Klaus Immelmann. Angus and Robertson, Sydney, 1966.

Budgerigars in Colour by A. Rutgers. Blandford, London, 1962.

Foreign Birds by Cyril H. Rogers. Foyles Handbook, London, 1954.

Parrot Guide by Cyril Rogers. Pet Library, London, 1969.

Parrots, Cockatoos and Macaws by Edward J. Boosey. Rockliff, London, 1956.

Penguins by Bernard Stonehouse. Golden Press, New York, 1968.

Poultry Keeping by L. C. Turnhill. Young Farmers' Club booklet No. 5 written for the National Federation of Young Farmers' Clubs.

The Handbook of Foreign Birds Vol. 1 & 2 by A. Rutgers. Blandford Press, London, 1964.

The Pan Book of Home Pets by Katherine Tottenham. Pan Books, London, 1963.

The Parrots of Australia by W. R. Easman and A. C. Hunt. Angus and Robertson, Sydney, 1964.

Waterfowl in Australia by H. J. Frith. Angus and Robertson, Sydney, 1967.

What Bird is That? by Neville W. Cayley. Angus and Robertson, Sydney, 1966.

INDEX

Page numbers in bold type refer to illustrations.

SOME OTHER TITLES IN THIS SERIES

Natural History

The Animal Kingdom
Animals of Australia
  & New Zealand
Bird Behaviour
Birds of Prey
Evolution of Life
Fishes of the World
Fossil Man

A Guide to the Seashore
Life in the Sea
Mammals of the World
Natural History Collecting
The Plant Kingdom
Prehistoric Animals
Snakes of the World
Wild Cats

Gardening

Chrysanthemums
Garden Flowers

Garden Shrubs
Roses

Popular Science

Astronomy
Atomic Energy
Computers at Work
Electronics

Mathematics
Microscopes & Microscopic Life
The Weather Guide

Arts

Architecture
Jewellery

Porcelain
Victoriana

General Information

Flags
Guns
Military Uniforms
Rockets & Missiles
Sailing

Sailing Ships & Sailing Craft
Sea Fishing
Trains
Warships

Domestic Animals and Pets

Budgerigars
Cats
Dog Care

Dogs
Horses & Ponies
Pets for Children

Domestic Science

Flower Arranging

History & Mythology

Discovery of
  Africa
  North America
  The American West
  Japan

Myths & Legends of
  Ancient Egypt
  Ancient Greece
  The South Seas